MACHINE LEARNING

TABLE OF CONTENTS

MACHINE LEARNING FOR BEGINNERS
The Absolute Beginner's Guide to Learn and Understand Machine Learning Effectively

MACHINE LEARNING WITH PYTHON
A Step-By-Step Guide to Learn and Master Python Machine Learning

MACHINE LEARNING

FOR

BEGINNERS

The Absolute Beginner's Guide to Learn and Understand Machine Learning Effectively

Introduction

Congratulations on purchasing *Machine Learning: The Absolute Beginner's Guide to Learn and Understand Machine Learning Effectively and* thank you for doing so.

We are living in very exciting times. Times when everything around us is changing. If you have been fortunate enough to have been out of school for several decades you're probably looking at the world with slack jaws, mouth agape, and eyes wide open in surprise at the way things have evolved. If you thought computers were exciting an innovative a few decades ago, the concept of "machine learning" may have you overwhelmed.

But, life is even more exciting for the young person just starting out. To you, the concept of machine learning is an adventure to be embarked upon. It's a time when the fantasy that spurred our imaginations has begun to turn science fiction into reality. So, when you hear terms like artificial intelligence, machine learning, and neural networks, your mind can't help but to drift toward action-packed movies with life-like cyborgs bent on taking over the world.

While the reality is far from the likes of the stories we have been told, machine learning is definitely a part of our present and our future. In this book we will begin to sift the wheat from the chaff, dividing non-fiction from those imaginary characters and bring the reality of new technology to life in ways previous generations could have never imagined.

When applied in the right way, machine learning has the capability of changing the lives of billions of people. In this book, we will break down the very basics of what this new technology is so that even the virgin computer programmer will be able to understand. We will discuss...

- What exactly is machine learning and why should we care

- How neural networks actually work

- What all of it has to do with deep learning

- Algorithms and what they can do

- Different machine learning applications - their advantages and disadvantages

- What's in store for all of us in the future

There is no doubt that we are on the precipice of some great things in technology. The fevered excitement behind it is probably the biggest technological advancement of our present time. Already, it has impacted our lives without us realizing it. Companies we do business with regularly (Apple, Amazon, Facebook, Google, Netflix and more have heavily invested in finding new applications, many already in place, to benefit how consumers interact with them.

Think about how fast a search engine can find what you're looking for online giving you thousands (if not millions) of options within a fraction of a second. How about the spam filters you use with your emails, designed to learn your preferences and then intercept suspicious activity before it does you harm, or perhaps a computer with the ability to identify abnormal activity on your bank account. This list goes on.

Most of us have become completely unaware of how machine learning has slowly crept into our lives in many ways and will continue to impact us in the years to come. In fact, it has made a major impact on dozens of applications that we use every day.

4

As a beginning student of machine learning, you have a lot to look forward to, now and well on into the future. While we're not at the stage of the "Terminator" and big corporations like Cybernetics yet, machine learning is the future and something we all must know about. If you've picked up this book, then you're already keen to be a part of this new revolution. Well, hold on to your seatbelts because we're about to go on a bumpy ride.

There are plenty of books on this subject on the market, thanks again for choosing this one! Every effort was made to ensure it is full of as much useful information as possible, please enjoy!

Chapter 1

An Introduction to Machine Learning

You probably already have a pretty good idea of what machine learning is but maybe the explanations you've gotten are just a little bit cloudy. You know it's a key component of artificial intelligence but even that definition is a little fuzzy. It can be very difficult to wrap your head around the concept. It helps to understand that the foundation of Machine learning lies firmly rooted in our own biology.

For eons, we've viewed the human brain as the only creation with the ability to learn and process information from complex data. Now, we're told that inanimate objects can learn and change their behavior through this new innovation. It boggles the mind to think of it that way. However, there is a good reason why it is not only possible but is already a major part of how we live and do business today.

What is It?

To put it in the simplest of terms, machine learning is the art of computer programming that allows the computer to learn and to automatically adjust its functions to perfect how well they accomplish their task. A computer with machine learning capabilities can actually improve their performance based on their own experience without having an explicit program to tell them exactly what to do.

This process of learning actually begins with the ability of the program to observe collected data and compare it with previous data to find patterns and results and adjust itself accordingly. All of this is done through a complex system of neural networks and algorithms working together in order to produce the desired results. In essence, it means that computers are slowly beginning to learn to think like humans, learning from their experiences and changing in order to improve the results they pick up.

This is done in a wide variety of ways which we will discuss in later chapters of this book. It is now one of the most effective means of simplifying work that has to be done. By reducing the need for every program to be written for every possible function a machine can do, it allows the machine to teach itself how to perform the work done in a faster and more efficient manner.

If you're not quite sure how this works, let's use an example. Suppose you need to create a program that requires the computer to filter out certain types of data. In the traditional programming method, you would have to 1) have a human examine what data you want to be eliminated and then compile a list of ways that unwanted data might appear and identify the specific patterns that may appear. 2) Then the human would have to write a specific algorithm created to teach the computer exactly what to look for. 3) The human would then have to develop a software program that could identify those patterns and other details and label them accordingly. 4) Test the program and find any anomalies that could create a problem in finding the unwanted data and then go back to step one and repeat the process over and over again until the program is actually perfected.

Even with this pretty basic list of steps, you would only be able to program the computer to complete one task and would have to repeat the process for any other task that you also may need the computer to do. To complete all of these tasks, you will have to comply with an extensive list of rules in order for it to work correctly. This leaves your programming efforts open to errors popping up and disrupting the whole process. However, if you had chosen to use machine learning to accomplish the same thing, the process would have been done much more quickly with less risk of errors developing.

In addition, once the program is updated using the traditional method, the designer of the program could never feel like the job is done. He (or she) will always have to periodically go back and update it on a regular basis to ensure that it is compatible with the latest technology being used at the time. This would have to be done repeatedly until it is replaced by another program altogether.

Machine learning is a technique that once uploaded will run itself. It will automatically tell when updates need to be made and can even latch onto a system and get its own updates, freeing up the human to do other things. Machine learning makes it possible to solve even the most complex of problems with minimal human interference. Depending on the type of machine learning you use, once its live and active in the system, the machine can continue to make its own adjustments and recognize its own failures and successes for as long as it remains that way.

There are many advantages to using machine learning in computer programming today but no doubt there will be many more new ways to use it in the future. Right now, it is primarily used to…

- Solve problems that involve long lists of rules

- Solve very complex problems that do not have any apparent solution

- Adapt to new data in non-stable environments

As more and more people become aware of how great machine learning can be, it is likely that it will be used in hundreds or thousands of other purposes. In time, it is feasible that it will be used in every industry in existence and may be used at some point to even create new ones.

Types of Machine learning

There are several different types of machine learning that can be used right now, each used to accomplish a different type of problem and every day new approaches to it are being published. When looking at different types of machine learning (ML) programs, they can all be categorized in two different ways; by form or function.

ML learning style programming can be either supervised or unsupervised and the form of function can be any type of classification, regression, decision tree, clustering, or deep learning type program. Regardless of the type used, all ML programming must contain the following:

- Representation: consisting of a group of classifiers or a basic language that the computer can understand

- Evaluation: a means of taking data and scoring it based on the program's objective

- Optimization: a strategy that gets you from the input data to the expected output

These three components are the basis for any learning algorithms that will be used to program the machine learning techniques into the computer. The primary goal of these algorithms is to help the computer to generalize and process data beyond its original programming so it can literally interpret new data that it may have never worked with before.

Machine learning types can also be categorized based on whether or not they have been "trained" by humans. Supervised and semi-supervised training requires some level of human interface in order to work effectively, but unsupervised and reinforcement learning can pretty much work entirely on their own without human interference.

Other factors that could categorize them could be:

- How they learn
- How simple or complex they are

The fact is that there is a lot to learn about machine learning. It is an extremely versatile program that can be applied in nearly every computer situation there is. However, before you can determine exactly which type of machine learning you will need, you'll have to first take a very close look at the problem you are facing and make your decisions from there.

It is true that deep learning has accomplished many things since it was first introduced. Because of its versatility and adaptability in so many situations, it has enabled computers to be able to detect speech patterns, create text-to-speech programs, retrieve information when needed, and even predict consumer usage in different industries. We have become more dependent on these programs than we may realize, and we are sure to see more of this cutting edge type of programming in the very near future in the field of healthcare, robotics, marketing, and more.

Supervised vs. Unsupervised Learning

A machine learning system can be labeled accordingly based on how much human interaction it needs to function. There are many different classifications for this but there are four primary categories you may see when studying machine learning basics: supervised, unsupervised, semi-supervised, and reinforcement learning. These labels are simply descriptions of the different ways that algorithms make it possible for machines to perform functions, make decisions, and analyze data. With each of these, the machine is expected to learn something from each task it performs. Let's begin by taking a closer look at what these categories actually are and how they work.

1) Supervised Learning

- In supervised learning, the machine is already programmed to expect a certain output of an algorithm in its system before it begins its work. In essence, it knows the kind of answer it is trying to reach, and simply needs to work out the different steps needed to find it. The algorithm is learned by a specialized set of training data that "guides" the machine to the right conclusion. So, if something goes wrong and the algorithms produce a result that is vastly different from the expected outcome, the training data previously entered will step in and redirect the functions so that the computer gets back on track.

- The majority of machine learning is supervised learning where the input variable (x) is the primary tool that is manipulated to reach the output variable (y) by using the different algorithms. All of this data - the input variable, the expected output, and the algorithm is provided by humans.

- Supervised learning can be categorized further into two different ways: classification and regression.

o When working with classification problems, all the variables are grouped together based on the output. This type of programming can be used in analyzing demographic data, i.e. marital status, sex, or age. So, if you are given a large number of images, each with its own set of identifying data, you could program the computer to analyze those images and acquire enough information to recognize and identify new images in the future.

o Regression works on problems that include situations where the output variables are set as real numbers. In this case, you could have a large number of molecules with varying combinations to make up different drugs. With supervised training, you could program the computer to analyze the data and then use it to determine if new molecules introduced into the system make up drugs or some other type of matter.

o There are many practical applications for classification and regression with supervised learning. Some algorithms can also be used for both but we'll discuss that in more detail later on.

- Some of the most commonly used algorithms used in supervised learning include:
  o K-nears neighbors
  o Linear regression
  o Neural networks
  o Support vector machines

- o Logistic regression

- o Decision trees and random forests

2) Unsupervised Learning

- Unsupervised learning is not as common as supervised learning but it is probably the most important aspect of machine learning that you will need. It is this type of learning will be the key to the effectiveness of artificial intelligence and other similar developments in the future. The basic concept behind unsupervised learning is to have the machine teach itself without human interference.

- With unsupervised learning, the system is not provided with any preexisting data and the outcomes of the problems are not already known. In other words, the program is working blind using only logical operations to chart its path to a decision. This makes problem solving under unsupervised learning very challenging, but it is this type of learning that is more closely linked to the way the human mind processes information.

- It is more often used as a means of predicting, interpreting, or finding solutions to an unlisted amount of data by taking the input data and analyzing it against the basic binary logo mechanism already included in every computer system.

- Unlike supervised learning, where data is fed into the system, the unsupervised learning model allows you to submit data for analysis with no previous existing information to base decisions on. For example, if you were to input an image with several different geometric shapes in it, the system would

13

analyze the image to learn as much as possible from it. It works on its own to identify the problem, classify what information it has, and then classify that information based on the different shapes, sizes, and colors and then labels it accordingly.

- Inevitably there will be wrong answers but with each wrong answer, it will go back and reanalyze the data and make the necessary adjustments. With each attempt to solve a problem, the degree of probability will be reduced.

- The value of unsupervised learning, however, lies in the machine's ability to recognize when it has made a mistake and how it adjusts its analysis to correct it.

- Some of the most commonly used algorithms in unsupervised learning include:

  o Clustering; K-means, hierarchical cluster analysis

  o Association rule learning: Eclat, priori

  o Visualization and dimensionality reduction

Supervised learning process: two steps

Learning (training): **Learn a model using the training data**
Testing: **Test the model using unseen test data to assess the**
model accuracy

$$Accuracy = \frac{\text{Number of correct classifications}}{\text{Total number of test cases}},$$

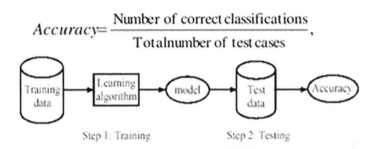

Step 1: Training   Step 2: Testing

3) Semi-Supervised Learning

Semi-supervised learning is merely a hybrid combination of both supervised and unsupervised. To understand it better, it helps to first understand the difference between the first two. With supervised learning, the algorithms are designed and trained based on datasets that have already been labeled by a human engineer. This data is used to guide the machine to the right conclusion. With unsupervised learning, the algorithms are not given any prelabeled data, so the system must analyze the data and determine what is important to them and draw its own conclusions. With semi-supervised learning, this difference is minimized, as the system is provided with a combination of both labeled data and unlabeled.

There are many reasons why one might choose this method. First, it is not always practical to label all the data that is needed for computer programming. Labeling millions of pictures is not only time consuming, it can also be extremely cost-prohibitive. In addition, complete interference by humans can run the risk of creating biases on the

15

computer model. To balance this out, offering a modest collection of labeled data during the training process and testing with unlabeled data seems to produce more effective and accurate results.

In many cases, it is the preferred option for situations like webpage classification, speech recognition, and for other extremely complex analysis like genetic sequencing. It allows you to access massive volumes of unlabeled data where the process of identifying and assigning labels would represent an insurmountable task.

4) Reinforcement Learning

This style of machine learning is very similar to what happens in a psychiatrist's office. The basic concept here is very similar to unsupervised learning in that it allows a great deal of control to be given to the software and the machines to determine what the appropriate action should be. Here, feedback is necessary in order to let the machine know if it is making progress or not so it can adapt its behavior accordingly.

The algorithms used here help the machines learn based on the outcome of the decisions they make. It is a complex system that relies on a large number of different algorithms working together to determine what happens next to achieve the desired results or to solve a specific problem.

When compared to other types of machine learning, the differences are made very clear. In supervised learning, there is a human supervisor who has the knowledge of the current environment and shares that knowledge in the form of data to help the machine to understand the problem and come up with the solution. However, there may be many subtasks that the system can perform without that human interaction. So, there are times when the computer can learn from its own experiences.

In both supervised and reinforcement learning, there is a function called computer mapping happening between the input data and the output data. But with reinforcement learning, there is an additional "reward" function that gives the system enough feedback so that it can gauge its progress and redirect its path when needed.

This same mapping function also exists in unsupervised learning. However, with unsupervised learning, the reward system does not exist. The primary focus of the machine is to locate patterns and identify properties rather than measuring progress toward an actual end goal. For example, if the machine is tasked to recommend a news report for the user, with reinforcement learning, the system will examine past feedback from the user and then create a graph of news reports that are in line with their past personal interests. But with unsupervised learning, it will look at past history and try to identify a pattern and select a report that matches with that particular pattern.

There are other types of machine learning that may not be as common or well recognized. These include batch learning, where the system is given all the data at one time, not in smaller increments; online learning where the system processes data in small increments or in small groups; instance-based learning, which is predominantly a simple memorization program; model-based learning where the system learns from examples and then is asked to make predictions.

It is important to understand that while machines can effectively learn, they are not like little tiny humans who already know how to tell the difference between a pineapple and an orange, or those that can, without much input, determine colors, shapes, sizes, etc. In order for machines to learn, they must have a great deal of quality data input even for the simplest of programs in order for them to be effective.

This means that a great deal of care must be taken when choosing the type of data you use to program the computer. If your data is not relevant, accurate, and reliable it will be full of errors that will make it very difficult for the machine to do its job. So, the key here is to make sure that you're giving it quality data and basing your algorithms on that data.

Chapter 2

Neural Networks

Those not directly involved in machine learning, the average Joe, would probably be very surprised to learn that they have already interacted with plenty of artificial intelligence and other forms of machine learning. Global leaders like Amazon, Apple, Facebook, Google, and IBM have spent millions of dollars on research and applications that will take their businesses to the next level.

Some of that research is already impacting us on a daily basis without us even knowing about it. A good example of this is every time you do a search on the internet, as soon as you insert a keyword into the search box, it is machine learning that scans the millions of websites and compiles a list of those sites that closely fit your search criteria.

You also see evidence of it in spam filters for your email, or on Netflix when it recommends the next shows for you to watch. It's used in the medical industry to classify medications, and it's a huge part of the Human Genome Project as it sifts through the billions of combinations of DNA patterns that may relate some hidden secret about your family history, health prospects, and risk factors.

These systems are highly sophisticated and can be adapted to every other industry that exists around us. All of them are made possible by the use of algorithms that are designed to guide the computer through various learning processes. With the right algorithm, a system can identify abnormal behavior that goes against a set pattern and teach itself to predict possible outcomes for a wide variety of situations.

These algorithms, data receptors and everything else that make all of this possible are contained within something called an artificial neural network. Since they were first introduced in the 1950's, they have been seen as a panacea for the future of science. Patterned after the human brain, their main role is to allow a machine to learn while in the training phase of programming and then use that knowledge to apply to future situations.

What are They and How They Work?

When you think of terms like deep learning, artificial intelligence, and machine learning it all refers to what is happening to the neural network. When we say the machine learns, it really means that the neural networks are being trained in the same way as the human brain.

A good way to think of these networks is to think of many simple parallel processors integrated with hundreds (or thousands) of tiny connections that make up a computational distributed model. In the human brain, there are millions of neurons all interconnected by synapses that allow them to make computations and analysis in the cerebral cortex. As these connections are made, learning is achieved allowing the person to acquire new skills so they can accomplish complex problems.

In neural networks, however, there are hundreds of homogeneous processing units that are interconnected through links. The beauty of the design is in its simplicity and in the unique configuration of the connections. The data is entered through designated input units and travels through several layers of units as it computes the problem until it reaches the output layer, which communicates a final decision that is to be carried out by the program.

In its earliest days, the structure of a neural network was extremely simple with only a few units to transmit information. Today though, a single network could conceivably have millions of units all intertwined and working together to recreate the learning process. The more modern networks are capable of solving extremely complex problems in a wide variety of areas.

The McCulloch-Pitt's Neuron - What is It?

We now understand that a neural network is a computer system that has been designed to mimic the way the human brain works. In fact, there are a lot of similarities between the human brain and an artificial neural network:

- They are formed by millions of artificial neurons, each able to compute and come up with a solution
- Each neuron (unit) has many weighted connections
- They are parallel and non-linear
- They are trainable - learning happens when the connections' weight changes
- They do not penalize the system for errors but can actually adapt to new knowledge
- They can produce outputs based on new input data they have never encountered before

On the surface, they work very similarly to the human brain but let's take a little time to look at how a single unit works. While all of the above describes how the entire neural network actually functions, the McCulloch-Pitt's neuron is the smallest part of a network.

In the human brain, a neuron is the smallest unit of mental processing there is. In an artificial neural network (ANN), this unit (the neuron) is the fundamental means of performing any type of calculation. It is comprised of three basic elements.

- The connections, characterized by weight or synaptic efficacy

- A summing agent that processes the input signals and their synapses to come up with a sum of linear combinations

- An activation function that limits the extent of the neuron's output

The McCulloch-Pitts (MCP) neuron was introduced in the early 1940s and was named after neuroscientist Warren S. McCulloch, and the logician Walter Pitts. Their goal was to try to understand exactly what happened in the human brain to produce the complex patterns and then mimic them by connecting many basic cells together.

In their original design, there were many limitations that prevented the machine from actually "learning." The design was very simple - the inputs were limited to either a zero or a one and the output was also limited to a zero or a one. Every input was either excitatory or inhibitory.

The function of the MCP neuron was, to sum up all the inputs. So, if an input value was one and it was excitatory (positive), another one was added. If it was one and inhibitory (negative), then a one was subtracted from the sum. This process was done for every input and then a total sum was determined.

If the result was less that a preset value, then the output would be zero, if it was more, then the output would be one.

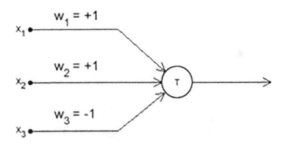

As you can see from the image, the data is represented with different variables. The variables W_1, W_2, and W_3, show which of the inputs are actually excitatory and which ones are inhibitory. If the subscript number is a positive one then that is an excitatory weight and if the number is a negative one it is an inhibitory weight.

The inputs are represented by the X weights at the beginning of the neuron (X_1, X_2, X_3). There are no limits to the number of inputs that could be included in the MCP neuron so the final sum of all the weights could vary widely from one situation to the next. However, if you think about it, it is possible to calculate the sum using the x's and the w's similar to the problem below.

$$Sum = X_1W_1 + X_2W_2 + X_3W_3 \text{ and so on.}$$

This type of equation is referred to as the "weighted sum."

When that sum is calculated, you can then check if the sum is $<$ or $>$ than T. If it is less than T, the output would be a zero, if it is more than T, the output would be 1. While this was a pretty basic concept, it wasn't long before people began to discover they could accomplish many amazing things with it as can be seen from the following examples.

NOR Gate

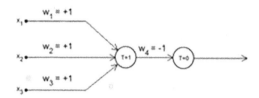

In the above example, you see what is called a NOR gate, which gives you an output of 1 because all the inputs are zero (X_1, X_2, X_3). You could experiment with different end case scenarios by varying the input from either zero or one.

In the above example, you have two neurons. The first neurons are the receivers and will accept the inputs you provide and the second is dedicated to working on the output of the first neuron. It is not involved nor does it have any access to any of the initial input data.

NAND Gate

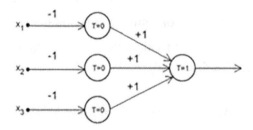

In the above example, you can see how a 3-input is created using the MCP neuron. A NAND gate will only give a zero if all the inputs are 1. The neuron in this figure needs 4 neurons. It takes the output of the first three inputs and uses it to create the input of the fourth.

The MCP neuron was extremely basic in its design but very effective in its approach. The MCP neuron is no longer in use today. This is mainly because the NOR and NAND gates already have extremely efficient circuitry so it was no longer necessary to use them in less efficient models. The goal was to use the interconnections in the best possible way.

Today, we have access to much more advanced neurons where the inputs can have even more practical uses. Now both neurons and their weights can have decimal values.

The model also had a threshold value that could influence the resulting effects based on whether it was positive or negative. In basic mathematical terms, this could be described as a "K" neuron which can be used in equations so they can actually process and calculate the sums, rather than just doing a check to see if it is less than or greater than the predetermined figure.

Neural Network Architecture

Within the neural network architecture, there are three basic types of activation functions at work. Threshold functions, which were commonly used in the McCulloch-Pitts neuron model, the Piecewise-linear functions, and the Sigmoid functions, which are more commonly used in the development of today's artificial neural networks. Neural Network Architecture gives a perfect balance between the linear and the non-linear behaviors as you can see in the example below:

$$\varphi(v) = \frac{1}{1 + e^{-a \cdot v}}$$

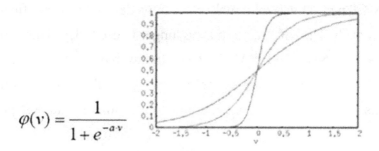

You can see here that the α is the parameter that shows the actual slope of the function.

The actual structure of the network architecture depends on which algorithm you are using. There are three separate classes of networks that can be used.

- One Layer Feedforward Networks: This is a very basic type of layered network. There are input knots and an output layer of neurons involved. The signal moves through the network starting at the input layer and moving linearly until it reaches the output layer. None of the connections will move back again through the system and there are no transversal connections that cut across any other connection in the output layer.

- Multilayer Feedforward Networks: These networks are slightly different in that they have one or more hidden layers that lie in between the input and the output layers. Each of these layers has connections that can receive incoming data from the previous layer and other connections that send output data to the next one. This way, a signal propagation happens in a linear fashion without the need of cycles or transverse connections. With this type of network, there is an increase in interactions between the different neurons giving it a broader and more global perspective.

26

- Recurring Networks: These networks function on a cyclical basis. The use of cycles can have a major effect on how a machine learns and on how it performs. The result is a much more dynamic system.

The process of machine learning is made possible by giving set parameters to a neural network and giving it the ability to adapt to various types of stimulation from its surrounding environment. This type of learning happens by the way the machine adapts to this stimulation.

Adaptations happen when a set of rules (or parameters) are given based on what is called a "learning algorithm." There are two fundamental kinds of learning algorithms that we have already discussed; supervised and unsupervised. Using these algorithms there are several different ways the machine can actually learn:

- Error Correction: When a neuron receives an input and generates a response, the machine knows what the desired response should be. If the machine makes a mistake it is given an error signal that will activate a control mechanism that will initiate a series of adjustments in the neuron so that the next response will be closer to the desired answer. In this method of learning, the machine will continue to process the data this way until it can produce the expected response.

- Memory-Based Learning: In this case, the machine stores all of its past experiences in its memory. Any correctly classified data is preserved and can be accessed. When a classification of data is needed on an experience the machine has never before encountered, it will access its data banks searching for related examples to process the new information. This type of learning is based on two fundamental factors: the basic ingredients and the criteria needed to define the test vector.

- o One example of this type of learning style is what is called the "nearest neighbor method" where the machine selects from its memory an example that is closest to the test subject.

- o There is also the k-nearest neighbor method where the neighborhood of the sample is not one but instead the set of k examples that are stored close together. With this method, the assigned class is based on the one that has the highest frequency surrounding the sample.

- Hebbian Learning: This method is based on the point when the A neuron's axon or its output transmission line is close enough to be excitable to neuron B. This will repeatedly and persistently cause an action potential triggering a growth process in one or sometimes even both neurons that will increase the efficacy of neuron A. All of this is based on two different rules:

- o If both neurons are connected by a synapse and are activated at the same time, then the weight associated with the synapse will progressively increase.

- o If both neurons are not activated at the same time then the weight of the synapse is progressively decreased and, in some cases, completely eliminated.

- This type of synapse is referred to as a Hebbian synapse. Based on the above rules when the correlation of the signals causes an increase in synapse efficacy, it can be referred to as a Hebbian modification. However, if it causes a reduction then it can be referred to as an anti-Hebbian.

- Competitive Learning: In competitive learning, the neurons are actually in competition with one another in an attempt to become active. Each neuron can only be active at a certain point in time. Competitive learning is comprised of three basic elements.

  o The neurons must all be identical. However, if there is a set of randomly generated synaptic weights, they will respond in a different way to the set of inputs provided.

  o There must be a limit to each neuron's strength

  o There has to be a mechanism in place that makes it possible for the neurons to compete for the chance to respond to the preset of inputs so that only one will be active at any given time.

  o The winner-takes-all neuron is the one that wins that right

- By using the neurons in a way that allows the user to specialize and tailor a set of similar inputs the machine can start to recognize set features of various classes of inputs. In its most basic form, the neural network would have only one layer of input neurons and one layer of output neurons, all connected together by input knots or synapses or forward excitatory connections. In more complex systems there may also be lateral inhibitions and inhibitory feedback connections at work as well.

Training the Neural network

When it comes to training a neural network, there are several different methods that have proven to be very effective. However, there is one method that seems to have the most positive results. The error propagation algorithm sometimes referred to as the error backpropagation. This method systematically adjusts the weight of all the different connections of the neurons. In this way, the responses can gradually get closer and closer to the preferred end result.

There are two stages to this type of training: the forward propagation, which is stage 1, and the back propagation or stage 2.

In stage 1, all the activated neurons from the very first layer all the way to the final layer are calculated. In this stage, the weight of the synaptic connections remains fixed. This means that with the first iteration the system will only use the default values. However, during stage 2, the actual answer from the network, the actual output will be compared to the expected output so that the actual error rate can be determined.

The resulting error rate is then propagated and reversed back to one of the synaptic connections where the weights are modified in an attempt to reduce the difference between the result and the expected output. The process is repeated until the error rate cannot be reduced any further.

- Forward Propagation: with forward propagation, input X enters the initial data that is then spread to the hidden layers of the system until it finally produces an output. The basic architecture of the network determines every aspect of this data including its depth, width, and activation functions. The depth shows how many hidden layers there are, the width shows how many units on each layer and the activation functions tell the system exactly what to do.

- Backward Propagation: utilizes a supervised learning algorithm that allows the weight of the connections to be adjusted with the sole purpose of reducing the difference in value between the current solution to a problem and the expected solution.

There are many advantages to training neural networks and utilizing them in machine learning. It is a highly innovative field of study and has a great deal of potential in the future of computer science.

- They are capable of solving problems that require answers that result in a degree of error

- They can generalize and produce answers to problems that they have not been trained for

- They can be easily implemented by defining a neuron, duplicating, and creating the associated connections

- They can compute operations quickly because every neuron uses only the value it receives as input

- They can produce stable outputs related to the input values

- They can evaluate all inputs at the same time to produce a result

Still, even with all those advantages, neural networks do have a few drawbacks that can make things more complicated.

- Its function can be similar to that of a black box; you can't go back and understand why it produced the result it created. You can only determine what happened.

- The memory cannot be localized within the network nor can it be described

- Because of their unique computer needs, they can only be used on those computers that have compatible hardware

- They do require extensive training techniques that can use up an extensive amount of time to produce the proper calculations

- They can only solve problems if they have been given the right algorithm to do it

- The output values can vary in their accuracy

- They require a large number of examples in order to create a good learning process to produce the right solution.

Neural networks are completely capable of independent decision making based on the number of inputs and variables. Because of this, they are able to create an unlimited number of recurring iterations to solve problems without human interference. When we see these networks in action, you'll find a numeric vector that represents the various types of input data. These vectors could be anything from pixels, audio and/or video signals, or just plain words. These vectors can be adjusted via a series of functions producing an output result.

Clearly, there is much more involved in neural networks than meets the eye. They can handle very basic problems and more complex problems using the same system. The only difference is the number of weights that are applied to the input values.

Chapter 3

How It All Relates to Deep Learning

All this technical information can be very exciting for the right person. We've entertained the thought of machine learning since the early days of science fiction. The idea of creating a machine that can learn enough to adapt its behavior is utterly fascinating. Still, it is important to get a full grasp of deep learning and its various applications we can already use in real life.

We know a neural network is designed to give you the same response when the same input values are entered. It has no memory to speak of but when the input has been given, it will react the same way to it every time. We call this behavior a stateless algorithm.

In most instances, this is all we need for a computer to function. However, it has its limitations. What happens when data is entered that has some variations in value and is not the same? For example, if you were asked to predict something that was about to happen, how would you go about it? You might access your previous memories and experiences stored in your mind to gauge the probability of certain events repeating themselves. You may not be able to guess with one hundred percent accuracy, but you could narrow down your options to several logical choices.

However, what happens when you are expected to guess events at random with only a few events that are precursors to the event you want to predict? In such a case, you would analyze the events prior to the expected event and determine the probability of what would happen next. In the human brain, it is pretty easy to determine possibilities when we know the sequence of events that came before. There are many clouds in the sky, with each passing hour the clouds are getting darker and darker. The temperature begins to drop, and the wind begins to increase in intensity. The logical probability here is that a storm is approaching.

With a neural network in deep learning, before this can happen memory must be added to the system. Anytime you need a response from the program, you will have to save a series of calculations that can be reused as input each time this problem comes up. So, with each problem solved, the computer will grow in its experience and knowledge so that it can adapt its predictions based on a growing body of knowledge.

This basic concept is referred to as a recurrent neural network, where the system actually goes through an upgrade each time it is used. This makes it possible for predictions and responses to vary based on new data and experiences. Over time, this can lead to the system recognizing patterns and other variables as long as the memory supports it.

We see this kind of application working in machines we interact with every day. A perfect example of this is your smart phone. When you are sending a text message you are automatically given a series of options to suggest the next word you might want to write. When you surf the internet, you are often given suggestions and advertisements based on past websites you've visited. We are often given recommendations for things to buy, movies to watch, foods to eat, and even places to go. All these things are the result of this kind of predictive algorithms that are used in deep learning.

The only difference is that eventually, predictions will be more extensive and not simply a word or a suggestion. With deep learning, it can one day be possible for entire stories to be written using neural networks. Eventually, recurrent neural networks will be able to match the style and practices of human brains in a vast number of ways.

How Does it Work

As we have already seen, learning happens when a machine makes a wrong prediction and must adjust its variables to minimize the percentage of error. Without some type of feedback that lets the machine know its error rate, this type of adaptation is impossible. There must be a way for the error to be fed back into the system, analyzed, and understood in order for the corrections to be made.

When a neural network is first initiated, the values of the different arrays and their weights are usually randomly assigned and adjusted as the machine receives its error feedback. This highlights the true purpose of the neural network: to rearrange after each iteration, the values of the weights in order to create a prediction that is closer to the expected output.

While this may seem logical and simple when it comes to the human mind that is naturally designed to do this in a fraction of a second, getting a machine to do it is not all that easy. The process of training an ANN to learn can be quite complex, especially when it comes to areas like speech recognition, self-driving cars, or computer vision. For this, you not only need all of the parts working as they should, but you will also need to generate a great deal of computational power and speed.

In recent years, this has been made possible by the use of graphics cards, which have allowed for new results to be used in parallel in order to speed up the process of computer predictions.

For a neural network to perform properly it must have quality raw data that can be extracted from the input. This data must be analyzed and packaged so that the machine is able to pull out any properties that could be of use in the learning process.

In the past, it required humans to manually identify these properties and input them into the machine. Basically, if the data was known it was fed into the neural network, then stored in its memory. This method of manually feeding data to the machine took up a lot of man hours to do. When the system received data that had already been received and analyzed before, it would recognize the similarities and store it as a past experience. So, by providing a wider variety of inputs, the machine could become more flexible in adapting information.

With deep learning, there is no longer a need for this type of human interaction, as the machine now has the capability of picking up the necessary raw data completely on its own. As more and more data is accumulated, the machine's ability to think and to learn improves.

The term "deep" is not to mean that the computer is in deep thought like a human, but it refers to the various levels of data received over time, each time allowing the system to learn and improve its performance, adding more depth of knowledge and experience. As this depth increases, the goal is to eventually develop the type of networks that can be 100% independent of human interaction.

Deep learning is a relatively new aspect of machine learning. This is because up until very recently, the kind of processing power and storage capabilities available were not sufficient enough to allow this type of learning to happen. However, now that it does exist and is readily available, this type of machine learning is becoming a new foundation of an entirely new form of technology.

As a result, deep learning has become the base foundation of all sorts of highly progressive artificial intelligence and can be applied in all types of areas. Already it is being used in speech recognition programs, image recognition, and self-driving cars. It is being applied in advanced robotics and has already been introduced in the medical imaging field as a means of making more accurate and reliable diagnoses of patients. It is used to operate drones, maintain other machines, and a host of other applications.

As a practical example of machine learning, let's take a look at how this ability can make a major change in one professional field. The primary role of a radiologist is to analyze thousands of radiographic images and make medical determinations. His expert eye is quickly able to spot anomalies such as a tumor or another foreign body that could be impacting a patient's health. If he makes a mistake, it could have severe consequences that could amount to life or death.

However, with deep learning software, the machine can examine millions of the same radiographic images and store them in its memory, never forgetting a single one. Its ability to analyze an image and extract similarities from the millions of similar images will allow it to give a much more accurate diagnosis of a patient's medical condition.

The same software could be adapted to other industries as well. The fact is that deep learning has the potential to change the world as we know it. We already rely on a GPS system to tell us how to get to a destination we have never been before. It is not a huge leap to having vehicles drive themselves. Machines can already analyze traffic conditions, signs, speed limits, obstacles and so on. The next evolution will be much, much more efficient than the clunky GPS systems we're using today.

Main Architecture

This area of machine learning is characterized by a system that works on more than one layer. Each layer is capable of receiving input from the one before it. With input received on each layer, the data is transformed, giving more insight to the machine. Therefore, the machine doesn't just learn with each problem it gives, but it learns on each layer of data as it passes through the system.

You might liken each layer to the different areas found in the human brain's cerebral cortex. The visual cortex, as an example, is responsible for not just seeing objects but has the ability to recognize them. This is the part of the brain that can identify images, recognize sequences, etc. In our brains, each of the sections has a very specific hierarchal order.

When our brain receives an image, it doesn't just immediately label it, but it processes it through several different stages. First, it must detect the edges, then it perceives the shape, and then it deciphers the colors, etc. Of course, all of this happens at the lightning speed of 13 milliseconds; if you're watching a movie it is about the speed of 75 frames a second. Neural networks, infused with deep learning, have a very similar hierarchal order. Even a simple network of three layers is now capable of distinguishing things in all kinds of environments and situations.

As data passes through the different layers it can select different aspects of the data and disregard those details that do not apply to the problem it is working on. There are several different types of deep learning networks:

- Discriminatory Feedforward Models: used to classify data

- Unsupervised Training: used to reconstruct the input and pre-train other models

- Recurring Models: used for sequencing, speech recognition, sentiment analysis, etc.

- Reinforcement Learning: used for machines that need to learn and mimic behaviors

It is clear that the algorithms and techniques used in deep learning make it possible for machines to find patterns, analyze situations, and identify regularities and irregularities in a wide range of areas. By doing so, it can actually help cut costs as it will no longer require input to be provided by humans. With so many thousands of input data becoming a part of this type of software, it is now possible that the computer has learned enough to automatically extract the data it needs entirely on its own. There's no telling what we will be able to expect in the future when it comes to the capabilities of a deep learning network.

Chapter 4

Algorithms

At its most basic level, machine learning is the use of different preprogrammed algorithms that collect and analyze data in order to determine possible outcomes within an acceptable range. Each time these algorithms receive new data the system learns and adapts to improve performance.

We've already touched on some of the most commonly used categories of algorithms: supervised, semi-supervised, unsupervised, and reinforcement, but now we're going to take a closer look at what an algorithm actually is, and some of the more popular types that can be used in machine learning.

Basically, an algorithm is a sequence of steps that will allow a machine to accomplish a specific task. It is important to point out here that while we refer to computers as using algorithms, they are not just limited to these types of machines. Other devices can also make use of algorithms as well.

There are three core characteristics that are contained in all algorithms:

- They must be finite: it has to have an end
- It has to have clear instructions
- It must be effective

Algorithms are mathematical entities, and while they are so much a part of modern technology, it is difficult to believe that they have already been in use for thousands of years. Archaeologists and historians have discovered records of them dating as far back as 1600 BC. These mathematical formulas can be applied in a wide range of settings.

Commonly Used Algorithms You Should Know

While there are hundreds of algorithms that can be used in machine learning, this chapter is going to focus only on those needed for computing software. Below we have some of the most commonly used algorithms, their purpose, and how they can be applied.

Linear Regression

Linear regression is probably the most well-known of all the algorithms associated with machine learning. The fundamental concept of this algorithm is to find the path that best models the linear trend, or in other words, finding the line that best fits the problem. It assumes that a linear relationship exists between the different input variables.

When there is only one input variable (x), the method used is called a simple linear regression but if there are multiple input variables, the method is referred to as multiple linear regression.

The very nature of a linear algorithm is to combine a specified group of input variables where the solution is an actual predicted output. In such cases, both input and output values have to be numeric in nature.

Each input value is given a single scale factor called a coefficient. It can be identified by the capital Greek letter Beta (B). Another coefficient is added so the line has another degree of freedom allowing it to move up or down along a two-dimensional plot line. This is referred to as the bias coefficient.

Y + B0 +B1*X

When there are higher dimensions and you're working with additional inputs it is referred to as a hyper-plane.

If a coefficient is zero it cancels out the effect of the input variable. This type of scenario is relevant in conditions where you need a means of regulating the changes and adaptations within the neural network. There are several ways linear regression can be applied.

- Simple Linear Regression can be used when you have single input variable used to estimate coefficients. It allows you to calculate statistical properties extracted from the input data like means, deviations, correlations, and covariance.

- Ordinary Least Squares are used when you have more than one input and you need to estimate the values of the coefficients. It treats the data as a matrix and applies linear algebraic operations to perform the estimations.

- Gradient Descent is used when you have multiple inputs to process the values of the coefficients. It works by using random values for every coefficient. The sum of the errors is then calculated for the input and output values to determine a learning rate. This is then used as a scale that can help to update the results in an effort to reduce the rate of error.

- Finally, there is regularization. These are extensions created to minimize the rate of error during the training phase, but they are also used to simplify the complexity of the model.

Logistic Regression

Logistic regression is very popular when you need to resolve binary classification problems. This is when the solution can be one of only two options. Sometimes referred to as dichotomy, it works well with problems that require either a true/false or yes/no answer.

To understand logistic regression better, you first have to have a clear understanding of linear regression. As an analyst, you must find the best line to show a specific trend. This requires finding an equation that gives the best direct feature that addresses the regression problem.

The standard practice is to use the least square method, where the idea is to shorten the distance between the line and the training data. Basically, the system is looking for a line that is "nearest" to all the input data.

Logistic regression is a part of a specific type of algorithm called the generalized linear model. Unlike with linear regression, your objective is to find a model that comes closest to the final value of the outcome or the variable. However, remember that you are solving a binary problem so there is no set value to predict. It is just a matter of two possible outcomes. You're actually looking for the higher probability that one outcome will actually occur.

Problems that linear regression would solve: How many inches of snowfall will we get this year?

Problems that logical regression would solve: Will it snow tomorrow?

Decision Trees

Decision tree algorithms are more often used to classify a model and label it in a tree structure. Many analysts find them to be excellent tools that can give them accurate and reliable output data.

Decision trees are easy to read and understand. In fact, when using them you will be able to see exactly why you need certain classifiers in order to make a decision. If you are new to writing code this is probably the best algorithm to cut your teeth on.

These algorithms all have exactly the same approach; to breakdown the data into the smallest possible subsets (those that contain only one group of outcomes). The data is divided up based on whatever predictors are available. Then they group all subsets of the same class together. They will continue to do this until they have the smallest set of data possible.

Once this is accomplished, it is very easy to make a prediction as to the expected behavior. Making this type of prediction is very simple. All the system does is follow the path that matches the given predictors. It will lead to the subset that contains all the yes answers.

Support Vector Machines

Support Vector Machines or SVM, are algorithms that can be used like weapons. Unlike the others mentioned, SVMs can come up with solutions that are far more precise than any of the others we've talked about.

This type of algorithm is extremely complex and utilizes some of the most challenging mathematical equations there are. Because of this unique complexity, SVMs can only slice through very small amounts of datasets. So, if the initial training data is too extensive, it is likely that SVM is not the best option.

SVMs are used for classifications. It searches for the optimum dividing line between all the different classes of data the system may be considering. In short, it looks for the widest separation (or margin) of data that exists between all the many groupings or subsets available.

Naive Bayes

The Naive Bayes algorithm uses statistical modeling to perform classification problems. It is relatively simple, but it can provide very precise solutions when used in the right way. It is very scalable when compared to the support vector machines, probably the most complex of all the algorithms in use today.

Naive Bayes is based on the Bayes' Theorem that assumes that "all predictors are independent of each other."

This algorithm does not store any data in its memory, but it does study and analyze the training data and uses that knowledge to adapt accordingly.

In real life, all predictors are interdependent but with Naive Bayes, they are all viewed as separate and distinct from each other (naive). As the system analyzes the data, it assigns a probability to each of the predictors associating them each with a specific class that is independent of any other features. This is referred to as the "class-predictor probability.

As an example, consider how it would analyze and determine the class of a specific fruit. It might first analyze and determine that the fruit is red. The algorithm then taps into its knowledge of fruits and determines that there are red apples, cherries, and strawberries.

When it looks at the next classification, shape, it determines that the shape is round. Apples, oranges, and peaches are all round, but strawberries are not. Finally, it will look at the size in diameter. In this prediction, the fruit is 3" in diameter. This could now be an apple, an orange, a peach, or a pomegranate. Once all of the different characteristics are considered, it will assign a percentage of probability that the fruit is from several classes with the one with the highest percentage being the one most likely to fit the set parameters. It could look something like this:

Probability of Apple   80%

Probability of Orange 10%

Probability of Strawberry 5%

…and so on.

If you have studied algorithms before, one of the first things you learn is that there are hundreds and perhaps thousands of them. Machines can learn based on the algorithm you use. With the right algorithm, machine learning is not only likely but extremely possible.

Chapter 5

Machine learning Applications

For anyone new to machine learning, the phrase "artificial intelligence" is probably the first term you can identify with. Believe it or not, it is not a thing of the future but already exists right now, today in many areas of life. This is because there are countless applications that can take advantage of this amazing type of programming in everyday life.

Right now, many of us are already using applications like Apple's Siri, Amazon's Alexa, and Google's NOW. These serve as virtual personal assistants that will listen to your commands and execute the required behavior on their own. They help you to find information, remember past requests, and send out commands to other devices to perform certain actions.

Most virtual assistants are voice-activated and can recognize and understand exactly what you say without the need for you to key in the information to activate it.

They can also make predictions when you're commuting. They can gather traffic data, use GPS navigation, and check on accident reports. The information is then used to create a real time picture of your route to your destination complete with detours around heavy traffic sites or construction zones.

You might also see them used in video surveillance for security jobs; they are frequently utilized in social media, email filtering, customer support, refining online data searches, making product recommendations, and even in fraud detection.

There are many ways machine learning has not only been helpful but has made it possible for many more things to be done that weren't possible only a few years ago.

Machine learning and "The Cloud"

You can even see it appearing in "the Cloud," which is the primary home base for many different applications. In the past, this was far out of reach for most people and businesses that didn't have the finances to store this much computing data in their own network of computers, nor did they have the technical knowledge required to design the necessary models to use.

Today, however, sites like Google, AWS, and Microsoft offer many options for storing machine learning data in the cloud where it can now be accessible from wherever you are in the world as long as you have an Internet connection.

These companies also provide SDKs or software developer kits that allow a user to actually embed the function directly into their needed applications, and most support all programming languages. Today, you don't need to know all the technical programming languages or have a computer science degree to take advantage of the many things that machine learning can do. You can actually use them from within whatever application you're using, completely unaware that you are interacting with a learning machine.

There are drawbacks though. As advanced as this new technology may be, it has yet to be perfected. For example, if you're accessing a machine learning application in the cloud, it is pretty much limited to that cloud. This means that if your database is not stored, or you have access to the cloud that the application is in, it is virtually useless to you.

So, if you, the user, choose to use one cloud provider, you will probably also have to use that same provider for all your data storage in order to take advantage of the applications it provides. But if there is an application stored on another provider's server, you may not be able to use it to your advantage.

There is no question that machine learning has made major strides in our modern day. While it does have limitations, its capabilities far outweigh those limitations on many fronts. As more and more people become aware of machine learning and what it can do, it will become a real game changer for everyone on the planet in some form or fashion.

Hybrid Applications

When it comes to artificial intelligence, machine learning applications really start to excel. Applications in general, are designed to give devices a wide bit of diversity that otherwise would not be possible. But with AI, the capabilities are even more advanced.

This is possible with the use of hybrid applications. While this field is very limited in the here and now, the future holds a lot of promise in the coming years. What can we expect from hybrid applications? A good way to answer that is by comparing two AI-driven technologies that are already in use today: the IBM Watson and the Tesla Model S.

These two different types of hybrid applications may one day make the difference between the simple artificial intelligence we use today and those that will one day produce highly intelligent machines of tomorrow.

IBM's Watson for example, already used in the health care industry, is capable of sifting through massive amounts of data, learning just about anything that could be used to diagnose, treat, and monitor patient care.

While it can absorb these incredible amounts of data, as far as the decision making process, there is still much left to be desired. It still has yet to grasp abstract ideas and concepts. It is incapable of knowing what a patient is or what kind of impact a drug could have on a particular patient.

In contrast, the Tesla AI, used in automobiles, contains powerful software with features supported by a huge integration of cellular connectivity. It is the means by which we can have self-driving cars and gives machines the ability to meter identify potential threats in the environment.

Advantages and Disadvantages

Hybrid applications are the next cutting edge advancement in machine learning. There are many reasons why people are beginning to take such a keen interest in them.

- They have an undefined development so they can be adjusted to work on a variety of platforms.

- They are easier to maintain because they work with only one codebase.

- They can be developed easily in a very short period of time

- They can be cross-platform so they are easy to scale on different platforms and be used on different devices.

- They are less expensive

- Their components are interactive

Still, while they have made incredible strides in advancing the field of machine learning, they are not perfect. There are still several areas where they need to grow more in order to be the principle tool to use in the future.

- They tend to operate much slower because they are more often based on web tech.

- They have a poor UX. They are not yet capable of giving the user a full native experience.

Chapter 6

Where Do We Go From Here?

We have already established how wonderful it is and what it can do today. What's even more amazing is what it will be able to do in the future. Yes, the future looks very bright for so many reasons. Of course, there are many predictions (probably created by machine learning) of what we can expect, but chances are when the next evolution has passed, we'll probably all be utterly surprised, standing on the sidelines muttering, "I didn't know machines could do that!"

But what are the predictions for the future? What do we know now that we can confidently keep a watchful eye out for?

- Quantum Computing: Right now, machine learning is mostly in the field of problem solving. They manipulate and classify data at incredible speeds. In the future, quantum computers will be better equipped to manipulate high-dimensional vectors. They will accomplish this by using the hybrid training methods. By utilizing a blend of supervised and unsupervised algorithms, there will be a huge increase in the number of vectors resulting in a highly impressive rate of speed.

- Improved Unsupervised Algorithms: Their ability to discover hidden patterns in data on its own and self-learning techniques make it possible for unsupervised learning to be utilized more fully in the future. Machines of the future will be built smarter and mostly unsupervised.

- Collaborative Learning: They will have an enhanced ability to use other computational entities in a collaborative manner. This will allow them to produce better results than what is already being achieved now.

- Deeper Personalization: In the future, machines will know much more about you personally. While we may think this is very annoying and an invasion of our privacy, the feeble attempts used today will be greatly enhanced. Those frustratingly inaccurate recommendations will be a thing of the past, ending our frustrations with the whole process after all.

- Cognitive Services: No doubt, we will see many more intelligent features appear in even the most every day machines. Computer scientists are already working on emotion detection systems, speech recognition, vision recognition, and so much more.

No doubt, you will be able to think of many more possibilities for machine learning in the future, but as I said before, there is a good chance that the majority of the world will be surprised at what will come out.

Conclusion

Thank for making it through to the end of *Machine Learning: The Absolute Beginner's Guide to Learn and Understand Machine Learning Effectively.* Let's hope it was informative and able to provide you with all of the tools you need to achieve your goals, whatever they may be.

There is no telling where this technology will take us in the future. Right now it is one of the most talked about topics in the field of IT. This is primarily because of its amazing potential in so many areas.

If technology continues to improve at such a rapid rate, there is a good chance that in the not too distant future, machines themselves will be programming other machines. At that point, the best question to ask is not what machines will be doing in the future but what will we?

In the pages of this book, we have discussed many things. We've learned:

- What machine learning really is
- What are neural networks
- How it all relates to deep learning
- How algorithms have been used
- And the many different applications that are already using it

We hope that you have been able to learn some valuable gems of information that will inspire you to dig deeper into what is our inevitable future.

Finally, if you found this book useful in anyway, a review on Amazon is always appreciated!

MACHINE

LEARNING

WITH

PYTHON

A Step-By-Step Guide to Learn and Master Python Machine Learning

Introduction

D o you want to learn how to do machine learning with Python but you have problems getting started? In this book, you'll learn all the important topics that you need to know for you to implement machine learning with Python. You'll learn how to download, install Python, and get the best package for machine learning in Python. You'll also load a dataset and understand its structure using data visualization and summaries. If you are new to machine learning and looking to eventually launch a career in Python, this book was designed for you.

Python is a powerful interpreted language. Unlike other languages such as R, Python is a complete language and platform where you can apply both research and development production. Still, there are many modules and libraries which you can select from and generate different ways to perform each task.

Methods in machine learning are popularly used in a wide variety of fields such as engineering, sciences, physics, and computer systems. Additionally, it is also used by commercial websites for the recommendation system, advertising, and predicting the actions of a customer.

Machine Learning has popped out as a major engine of most commercial applications and research endeavors. But this particular branch does not exclude large research companies. In this book, you'll get an in-depth introduction to the field of machine learning from linear models to deep learning and reinforcement learning. You will understand the principles behind machine learning problems like regression, reinforcement learning, and classification.

Chapter 1

Python Basics

W elcome! Is this your first time to programming? If not, then we assume that you want to learn how to use machine learning with python. Also, you could be looking for information about why and how you can get started with Python. If you are an expert programmer in any language, it will be easy for you to pick up Python very fast.

Before you can get started in Python, you need to know how to install Python on your computer. Next, you need to know a few concepts about the language syntax to be able to read and understand the python code. This chapter will take you through all these. So, get ready to learn a few important things in Python language.

Installing

Nowadays, most UNIX and Linux distributions already come with a recent Python version installed. Even some HP Microsoft computers have Python already installed.

Download Python

Before you can get started with Machine Learning with Python, you must have Python installed on your computer, however, you might not need to download it.

So, the first thing to do is to confirm that Python is not installed by typing "Python" in a command window. When you see a response from a Python interpreter, it will consist of a version number in its original display. In general, any recent version will work because Python tries to maintain backward compatibility.

If you want to install Python, you might as well search for the most recent stable version. This version will have the highest number not marked as an alpha or beta release.

If you're running a Windows OS, the most stable Windows' downloads can be found from the Python for Windows page.

If you're running Windows XP, you'll find a complete guide to installing ActivePython at "Python on XP".

For those using a Mac, you can navigate to "Python for Mac OS X page."

For those using Debian or Ubuntu, you should install python2x and pythonn2.x-deve packages.

Syntax
Python programs are written with the help of a text editor and must have an extension .py. It is not a must to have the first and last line in Python programs but it can assign the location of python as the first line **#!/usr/bin/python** and become executable. Nonetheless, the command prompt is another environment from which you can run python programs by entering "python file.py". In Python, there are no semicolons and braces. It is a high-level language. So instead of braces, blocks are selected by selecting the same indentation.

First Python program
Usually, when you start to learn any programming language, your first program to write will be "Hello, World!". This is an easy program that prints "Hello, World!" For our first python program, you will learn how to write a program which adds two numbers.

A program that adds two numbers

```
# Add two numbers
num1 = 3
num2 = 5
sum = num1+num2
print(sum)
```

How does the above program work?

The first line of the program begins with a comment. Comments in python programming are written starting with #. Python interpreter and compilers ignore comments. The reason why comments should be applied in Python programming is to describe the function of the code. Furthermore, comments help any other programmer to understand the working of your code.

Variables and Datatypes

A data type, as the name suggests, is the category of data in different types. It defines a collection of values plus operations that can take place on those values. The explicit value used in our programs is a literal. For instance, 11, 30.22, 'pypi' are all literals. Each literal has a type linked to it. For example, 11 is an int type, 30.22 is a float type and 'pypi' is of type string. Often, the type of literal will determine the type of operations that can be done to it. The table below contains basic data types in Python.

Types of data	In Python we call them	Examples
Integers	int	12, -999, 0, 900000, etc
Real Numbers	float	4.5, 0.0003, -90.5, 3.0; etc
Characters	str	'hello', "100", "$$$", ""; etc

Python contains an inbuilt function called type () which is used to define the data type of the literal.

```
>>>
>>> type(54)
<class 'int'>
>>>
>>> type("a string")
<class 'str'>
>>>
>>> type(98.188)
<class 'float'>
>>>
>>> type("3.14")
<class 'str'>
>>>
>>> type("99")
<class 'str'>
>>>
```

The <class 'int'> describes that the type of 54 is int. Also, <class 'str'> and <class 'float'> shows that "a string" and 98. 188 is of type str and float respectively.

At first, you might say that "3.14" is of type float but since it is wrapped inside double quotes, it is definitely a string. In the same way, "99" is a string.

A sequence of character data is a string. The string type in Python is called str.

String literals can either be defined by single or double quotes. All the characters inside the opening and closing quotes are part of the string as shown below:

```
>>> "

"
```

Escape sequence in strings

There are times when you want Python to interpret a sequence of characters inside a string differently. This might happen in one or two ways:

- If you want to suppress the unique interpretation that specific characters are supplied within a string.

- You want to apply specific interpretation to characters contained in a string that is often taken literally.

You can do this by using the backslash (\) character. A backslash character in a string implies that one or more characters which follow it must be uniquely treated. This is called an escape sequence because the backslash will make subsequent character sequence to "escape" its normal meaning.

Boolean Type

Python 3 has a Boolean data type. Objects of Boolean type may contain one or two values, False or True.

```
>>> type(True)
<class 'bool'>
>>> type(False)
<class 'bool'>
```

Python expressions are evaluated in a Boolean context. This means that they are interpreted to represent false or truth. A true value in Boolean is described as "Truthy" while a false value is described as "Falsy."

The truthiness of an object of the Boolean type is open. This means that objects which are equal to True are Truthy, and those that are equal to False are Falsy. However, objects that are not of Boolean type can be evaluated in a Boolean context and determined to be true or false.

Python Variables

In the first Python program, you were introduced to Python variables. You briefly saw how you can define variables in Python and assign them some values. This section discusses more variables in Python.

Variables like in any other programming languages are used to store values. Also, you can use variables to access data and manipulate data.

Create a variable

If you want to create a variable in Python, you must use the assignment operator. The format shown below is applied when you want to create a variable.

```
variable_name = expression
```

An example can include:

number = 12.

This statement will create a variable called number and assign it the value 12. When the Python interpreter comes across this statement, it performs the following things behind the scenes.

1. Store the variable "12" in a given location in memory.

2. Make the variable number point to it.

The crucial thing to understand is that the variable number itself doesn't have any value, it only points to the memory location that contains the original value.

Another important thing to note is that when you assign a value to a variable, make sure that you write the variable name on the left side of the assignment (=) operator. If you fail to do this, you will get a syntax error.

Python always detects the type of variable and operations performed on it depending on the value it has. The programming jargon that describes this is called, Dynamic Typing. This means that you can use the same variable to refer to a different type of data that initially points to.

Any time you assign a new value to a variable, the reference to the previous value is lost. For instance, if the variable number is assigned the string "ten", the reference to value "12" is lost. At this point, there will be no variable that will point to the memory location. When this takes place, the Python interpreter will automatically remove the value from the memory through garbage collection.

If you try to access a variable before you assign a value to it, you will get a NameError.

Control Flow
The control flow in a program highlights the order of program execution. In a Python program, control flow is carried out by function calls, conditional statements, and loops. This section will deal with the If Statement, While and For loops.

If Statement
There are occasions which you may want to run certain statements if some condition holds, or decide the type of statements to run based on different mutually exclusive conditions. Python has the compound "If Statement" that is made up of "if", "elif", and "else" clauses. These compound statements allow you to conditionally create blocks of statements. Below is a general declaration of an If Statement.

```
if expression:
    statement(s)
elif expression:
    statement(s)
elif expression:
    statement(s)
...
else:
    statement(s)
```

Here, "elif "and "else" clause are optional. As a reminder, there are no switch statements in Python, this means that you need to apply "elif", "if", and "else" for conditional processing. Take a look at this example of an If program.

```
if x < 0: print "x is negative"
elif x % 2: print "x is positive and odd"
else: print "x is even and non-negative"
```

The While statement
In Python, a WHILE statement supports the repeated execution of a statement or even a block of statement which are under the control of a conditional expression. Take a look of a While syntax.

```
while expression:
    statement(s)
```

A While statement can also consist of an 'else' clause, 'break and continue' statements. Below is an example of a While program example in Python.

```
count = 0
while x > 0:
    x = x // 2                # truncating division
    count += 1
print "The approximate log2 is", count
```

The for Statement
The Python language also contains the for statement which supports repeated program statement execution. The for statement has an iterable expression to control the blocks of statements. Below is a general syntax of a for statement.

```
for target in iterable:
    statement(s)
```

Keep in mind that "in" is a keyword. It is part of the syntax of the For Statement but not associated with the "in" operator which is applied in the membership testing. A for Statement can have an else clause, break, and continue statements. Here is a general declaration form of a For Statement:

```
for letter in "ciao":
    print "give me a", letter, "..."
```

Data Structures
They are structures which assist in data storage. Data structures have a collection of data linked to each other. In Python, there are 4 built-in data structures. They are as follows:

- Tuple
- List
- Dictionary
- Set

66

Below is a detail description of each data structure.

List

A list describes data structures which have an ordered set of items. Consider a shopping list that has several items which you need to purchase. The only difference is that your shopping list has each item on a separate line.

However, in the case of a list in Python, you only need to separate your items with commas. The moment you create a list, you have the permission to add, remove, or search items in the same list. Since a list allows you to add and remove items, it is considered as a mutable data type. This means that you can change it anytime.

Quick Intro to Objects and Classes

To understand more about a list in Python language, it is good to quickly introduce you to the concept of objects and classes. A list is an example of objects and classes. So, if you are going to use a variable such as j and allocate it a value say integer 7, then it is important to look at it as if you are creating object j.

A class contains methods. Methods and functions are similar. However, methods are defined inside that class alone. Therefore, the only way to access a function is by having an object in that class. For example, in the Python language, you can join a method to a list class that allows the class of the object.

The Python language has the append method for a list class which permits the addition of an item to the end of the list. Classes in Python have fields which take the form of variables declared to be used in a specific class alone. This means that if you want to use these variables, you require to have an object of that class alone. You access fields with the help of a dotted notation. For example, mylist.field.

```
# This is my shopping list
shoplist = ['apple', 'mango', 'carrot', 'banana']

print('I have', len(shoplist), 'items to purchase.')

print('These items are:', end=' ')
for item in shoplist:
    print(item, end=' ')

print('\nI also have to buy rice.')
shoplist.append('rice')
print('My shopping list is now', shoplist)
print('I will sort my list now')
shoplist.sort()
print('Sorted shopping list is', shoplist)

print('The first item I will buy is', shoplist[0])
olditem = shoplist[0]
del shoplist[0]
print('I bought the', olditem)
print('My shopping list is now', shoplist)
```

Output:

```
$ python ds_using_list.py
I have 4 items to purchase.
These items are: apple mango carrot banana
I also have to buy rice.
My shopping list is now ['apple', 'mango', 'carrot', 'banana', 'rice']
I will sort my list now
Sorted shopping list is ['apple', 'banana', 'carrot', 'mango', 'rice']
The first item I will buy is apple
I bought the apple
My shopping list is now ['banana', 'carrot', 'mango', 'rice']
```

Here's how it works

There is the variable, "shoplist" which has information about a person planning to go to the market. The "shoplist" allows you to store strings of names of things which you plan to buy. However, you can add any type of object like numbers.

This program also has a 'for' loop which will support iteration in the list. You should have started to realize that a list is similar to a sequence. Notice how the end parameters are used to call a print function. This shows that you want to end the output with space rather than a normal line break.

Next, you should add an item to the list using the append method. Check whether the item is added using the print function.

There is also a sorting method in the program. The purpose of this is to sort the list. It is important to note that this particular method affects the list itself and it can't return an altered list.

The next thing is to complete purchasing the item from the market. This process is equivalent to removing an item from the list. You do this with the help of the del Statement. For this scenario, you need to describe the item found in the list which you want to remove. Then use the del Statement to remove it from the list.

After that, the del Statement removes it from the list. To remove an item in a list using Python, you just write the following line function del shoplist [0].

Tuple

Tuples store multiple objects. They are similar to lists except that they don't have a lot of functions like a list class. One great feature about tuples is that it is immutable like strings. This implies that it is hard to change the tuples.

If you want to define tuples, you have to describe items and separate them with commas. Tuples are best used in cases where the collection of values can't change. Take for example:

```python
# I would recommend always using parentheses
# to indicate start and end of tuple
# even though parentheses are optional.
# Explicit is better than implicit.
zoo = ('python', 'elephant', 'penguin')
print('Number of animals in the zoo is', len(zoo))
new_zoo = 'monkey', 'camel', zoo
print('Number of cages in the new zoo is', len(new_zoo))
print('All animals in new zoo are', new_zoo)
print('Animals brought from old zoo are', new_zoo[2])
print('Last animal brought from old zoo is', new_zoo[2][2])
print('Number of animals in the new zoo is',
    len(new_zoo)-1+len(new_zoo[2]))
```

```
Output:

$ python ds_using_tuple.py
Number of animals in the zoo is 3
Number of cages in the new zoo is 3
All animals in new zoo are ('monkey', 'camel', ('python', 'elephant', 'penguin'))
Animals brought from old zoo are ('python', 'elephant', 'penguin')
Last animal brought from old zoo is penguin
Number of animals in the new zoo is 5
```

Dictionaries
A dictionary is similar to an address book which you can search details of a person by selecting his or her name. In a dictionary, keys are joined with values. Keep in mind that the key must be unique and you can again use immutable objects for dictionary keys by either applying mutable or

70

immutable objects for the dictionary values. Remember that the key-value pairs in the dictionary don't have a fixed arrangement.

Example:

```
# 'ab' is short for 'a'ddress'b'ook

ab = {
    'Swaroop': 'swaroop@swaroopch.com',
    'Larry': 'larry@wall.org',
    'Matsumoto': 'matz@ruby-lang.org',
    'Spammer': 'spammer@hotmail.com'
}

print("Swaroop's address is", ab['Swaroop'])

# Deleting a key-value pair
del ab['Spammer']

print('\nThere are {} contacts in the address-book\n'.format(len(ab)))

for name, address in ab.items():
    print('Contact {} at {}'.format(name, address))

# Adding a key-value pair
ab['Guido'] = 'guido@python.org'

if 'Guido' in ab:
    print("\nGuido's address is", ab['Guido'])
```

```
Output:

$ python ds_using_dict.py
Swaroop's address is swaroop@swaroopch.com

There are 3 contacts in the address-book

Contact Swaroop at swaroop@swaroopch.com
Contact Matsumoto at matz@ruby-lang.org
Contact Larry at larry@wall.org

Guido's address is guido@python.org
```

```python
x = 50


def func():
    global x

    print('x is', x)
    x = 2
    print('Changed global x to', x)


func()
print('Value of x is', x)
```

Chapter 2

Introduction to Machine Learning

The focus of Machine Learning is to learn the nature of data and apply it to specific models.

Although ML is a field in computer science, it is not the same as the traditional computational methods. When you look at traditional computing, algorithms are described as a set of programmed instructions. These instructions provide solutions to a problem.

ML algorithms make computers to learn from data inputs and apply statistical analysis to display values found in a given range. Therefore, ML allows computers to create a model from a data sample so that it can permit the automation of decisions based on the type of data entered.

Nowadays, technology users hugely benefit from the idea of machine learning. For example, the facial recognition technology provides opportunities to social media networks so that their users can tag and share photos with their friends.

There is also the optical character recognition (OCR). This type of technology is applied in movies, shows, and e-commerce to suggest to users based on their preferences. If you know self–driving cars, they also depend on machine learning to move.

This chapter will take you through some of the most common ML methods of supervised and unsupervised learning, as well as popular machine learning algorithms. Additionally, you'll learn why you need machine learning and some of the programming languages used with machine learning besides Python. Furthermore, this chapter will also look at some of the biases associated with machine learning, and consider a few things to help reduce these types of biases when you build an algorithm.

Machine Learning Methods

When it comes to the field of machine learning, there are tasks which are categorized into different divisions. Most of these divisions depend on how learning is performed, or on the type of feedback delivered based on the system developed.

The most popular machine learning methods include supervised learning and unsupervised learning. For supervised learning, algorithms learn from the example of input and output data labeled by humans. On the other hand, unsupervised learning does not supply to the algorithm any labeled data, but the algorithm has to find the structure within its input data by itself. Here's a detail discussion of these methods.

Supervised Learning

For supervised learning, the computer has an example of input data to work on. The aim of this method is to allow the algorithm to "learn" by comparing actual output using a trained output to discover errors and alter the model. In other words, this method contains patterns which assist in predicting label values on extra data that is unlabeled.

For example, in supervised learning, you can feed an algorithm data with shark images and label them as fish. Also, you can feed it with images of oceans and label it like water.

After the algorithm is trained several times with this particular data, the algorithm must be able to differentiate unlabeled fish images and unlabeled ocean images.

One of the most popular use cases of supervised learning is the application of historical data to help forecast the statistical chance of an event to happen. It can use historical stock market data to predict future changes in the market. Additionally, supervised learning can help in the filtering of spam emails. Supervised learning makes it possible to classify untagged photos of dogs by using photos of dogs that have been tagged already.

Unsupervised learning

Unlike supervised learning where data is labeled, with unsupervised learning, you deal with unlabeled data. This means that it is the task of the learning algorithm to identify similar features in the data that it is supplied. Since unlabeled data is very popular compared to labeled data, techniques of machine learning are among the most valuable in the industry. The aim of unsupervised learning is very simple.

The largest application of unsupervised learning is within the transactional data. There can be a massive data set made up of customers and the products which they purchase, but since you are a human, you can't manage to extract meaning and similarity from customer profile and their purchase history.

The best time to apply unsupervised machine learning is when you don't have data on expected outcomes, like defining a target market for a new product that your business has never sold before, but if you are attempting to understand your consumer base, supervised learning is the right technique.

Machine learning approaches

Machine learning is highly linked to computational statistics. For that reason, if you have some knowledge of statistics, it is important to understand and apply machine learning algorithms.

If you are new to statistics, here are some definition of terms which are popularly used in detecting the relation found in quantitative variables.

Correlation. This describes the association that exists between two variables said not to be independent or dependent.

Regression. At the lowest level, it is helpful at determining the relationship between one independent and dependent variable.

The k-nearest neighbor

This particular algorithm is applied in the pattern recognition model. Pattern recognition model is used in classification and regression. The k is a positive integer. In both regression and classification, the input contains k closest training example in a specific space.

The KNN classification

When it comes to this method, its output belongs to the class membership. This assigns a new object the most popular class in the k-nearest neighbors. Take for example, when k = 1, the object has to be assigned a class which has one nearest neighbor. The diagram below describes this algorithm. The diagram has blue diamond objects and orange star objects. Just remember that they belong to two different classes. That is the star and diamond classes.

Once you introduce a new object to space such as a green heart, you'll need the learning algorithm to assign the heart into a particular class.

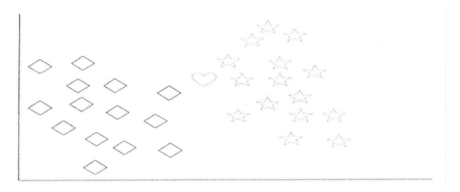

For k = 3, the algorithm will have to pick three nearest neighbors that belong to the green heart and assign it, either into the diamond or star class.

In this case, the three nearest neighbors of the green heart consist of the diamond and two stars. Therefore, the algorithm can label the heart that contains the star class.

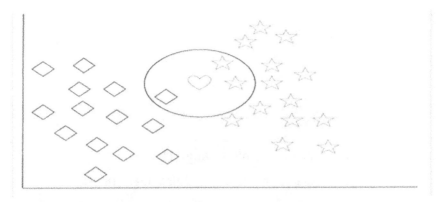

The k-nearest neighbor algorithm is among the basic machine learning algorithms labeled as "Lazy learning".

Decision Tree
In general, decision trees are important when you want to have a visual representation of decisions and display decision making. When working

with ML and data mining, decision trees are key when it comes to a predictive model. The model contains observations and creates a summary related to the target value of the data.

Learning in decision trees is important when you want to create a model that is useful at predicting a value depending on the input values.

If you take a look at a predictive model, the features of the data have to be defined using observation and represented by branches. Additionally, conclusions related to the data's target value are shown in the leaves.

This example demonstrates the various conditions that can show whether a person is supposed to go fishing or not.

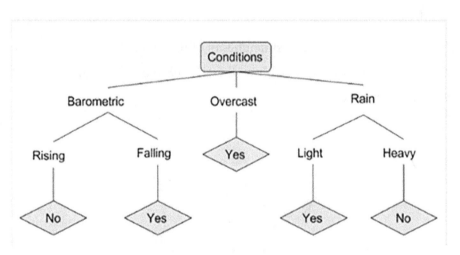

This decision tree is classified by sorting. Then it can display which classification is associated with a particular leaf. In the following example, it is a yes or no. The tree can then divide the day's condition based on whether it is correct to go fishing or not.

A real classification tree dataset will contain a lot more features compared to what is shown in this tree. All in all, 'relationship' will be easy to select.

Deep Learning

With deep learning, it will always try to copy the human brain and how it succeeds in processing sound and light stimuli. The underlining architecture of deep learning is powered by biological neural networks. Additionally, it contains many different multiple layers.

In the current machine learning algorithms, deep learning has succeeded in selecting most of the data as well as defeat humans in different cognitive tasks. Due to the following properties, deep learning is one of the best methods applied in AI.

Programming Languages

When a person wants to choose a language to use to learn with machine learning, there are few things that they may want to factor in such as the current status of job positions and the type of libraries available. Other languages that are used in machine language include C++, Java, and R.

Human Biases

While both data and computational analysis cause an individual to start to think like they aren't being objective, being biased on a given data doesn't mean that the output from the machine learning is neutral. The human bias affects the organization of data and algorithms that determine how ML should use data.

If you decide to use historical photographs of scientists in your specific computer training, a computer might fail to classify scientists.

Although machine learning is continuously applied in the business, biases that go unnoticed can lead to a systematic problem that can prevent people from receiving loans and many other things.

In short, human biases can negatively impact other people. This is very important to underline and work towards removing it as possible. One particular method which you can use to achieve zero biases is to ensure that several people work on a project. Since machine learning is an area which is continuously being improved, it is essential to remember that algorithms, approaches, and methods continue to change.

Chapter 3

Data Processing, Analysis, and Visualization

Understanding Data Processing
Data processing is the act of changing the nature of data into a form that is more useful and desirable. In other words, it is making data more meaningful and informative. By applying machine learning algorithms, statistical knowledge, and mathematical modeling, one can automate this whole process. The output of this whole process can be in any form like tables, graphs, charts, images, and much more, based on the activity done and the requirements of the machine.

This might appear simple, but for big organizations and companies like Facebook, Twitter, UNESCO, and health sector organizations, this whole process has to be carried out in a structured way. The diagram below shows some of the steps that are followed:

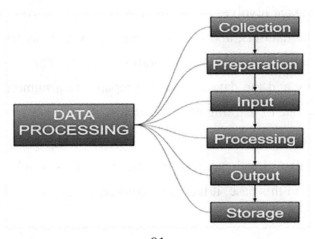

Let's look in detail at each step:

Collection
The most important step when getting started with Machine Learning is to ensure that the data available is of great quality. You can collect data from genuine sources such as Kaggle, data.gov.in, and UCI dataset repository. For example, when students are getting ready to take a competitive exam, they always find the best resources to use to ensure they attain good results. Similarly, accurate and high-quality data will simplify the learning process of the model. This means that during the time of testing, the model would output the best results.

A great amount of time, capital, and resources are involved in data collection. This means that organizations and researchers have to select the correct type of data which they want to implement or research.

For instance, to work on the Facial Expression Recognition requires a lot of images that have different human expressions. A good data will make sure that the results of the model are correct and genuine.

Preparation
The data collected can be in raw form. Raw data cannot be directly fed into a machine. Instead, something has to be done on the data first. The preparation stage involves gathering data from a wide array of sources, analyzing the datasets, and then building a new data set for additional processing and exploration. Preparation can be done manually or automatically and the data should be prepared in a numerical form to improve the rate of learning of the model.

Input
Sometimes, data already prepared can be in the form which the machine cannot read, in this case, it has to be converted into readable form. For

conversion to take place, it is important for a specific algorithm to be present.

To execute this task, intensive computation and accuracy are required. For example, you can collect data through sources like MNIST, audio files, twitter comments, and video clips.

Processing
In this stage, ML techniques and algorithms are required to execute instructions generated over a large volume of data with accuracy and better computation.

Output
In this phase, results get procured by the machine in a sensible way such that the user can decide to reference it. Output can appear in the form of videos, graphs, and reports.

Storage
This is the final stage where the generated output, data model, and any other important information are saved for future use.

Data Processing in Python

Let's learn something in python libraries before looking at how you can use Python to process and analyze data. The first thing is to be familiar with some important libraries. You need to know how you can import them into the environment. There are different ways to do this in Python.

You can type:

Import math as m

From math import *

In a first way, you define an alias m to library math. Then you can use different functions from the math library by making a reference using an alias m. factorial ().

In the second method, you import the whole namespace in math. You can choose to directly apply factorial () without inferring to math.

Note:

Google recommends the first method of importing libraries because it will help you tell the origin of the functions.

The list below shows libraries that you'll need to know where the functions originate from.

NumPy: This stands for Numerical Python. The most advanced feature of NumPy is an n-dimensional array. This library has a standard linear algebra function, advanced random number capability, and tools for integration with other low-level programming languages.

SciPy: It is the shorthand for Scientific Python. SciPy is designed on NumPy. It is among the most important library for different high-level science and engineering modules such as Linear Algebra, Sparse matrices, and Fourier transform.

Matplotlib: This is best applied when you have a lot of graphs which you need to plot. It begins from line plots to heat plots and you can apply the Pylab feature in IPython notebook to ensure plotting features are inline.

Pandas: Best applied in structured data operations and manipulations. It is widely used for data preparation and mining. Pandas were introduced recently to Python and have been very useful in enhancing Python's application in the data scientist community.

scikit-learn: This is designed for machine learning. It was created on matplotlib, NumPy, and SciPy. This specific library has a lot of efficient tools for machine learning and statistical modeling. That includes regression, classification, clustering, and dimensionality community.

StatsModels: This library is designed for statistical modeling. Statsmodels refers to a Python module which permits users to explore data, approximate statistical models, and implement statistical tests.

Other libraries

- Requests used to access the web.

- Blaze used to support the functionality of NumPy and Pandas.

- Bokeh used to create dashboards, interactive plots, and data applications on the current web browsers.

- Seaborn is used in statistical data visualization.

- Regular expressions that are useful for discovering patterns in a text data

- NetWorx and Igraph applied to graph data manipulations.

Now that you are familiar with Python fundamentals and crucial libraries, let's now jump into problem-solving through Python.

An exploratory analysis in Python with Pandas

If you didn't know, Pandas is an important data analysis library in Python. This library has been key to improving the application of Python in the data science community. Our example uses Pandas to read a data set from an analytics Vidhya competition, run an exploratory analysis, and create a first categorization algorithm to solve this problem.

Before you can load the data, it is important to know the two major data structures in Pandas. That is Series and DataFrames.

Series and DataFrames

You can think of series as a 1-dimensional labeled array. These labels help you to understand individual elements of this series via labels.

A data frame resembles an Excel workbook and contains column names which refer to columns as well as rows that can be accessed by row numbers. The most important difference is that column names and row numbers are referred to as column and row index.

Series and data frames create a major data model for Pandas in Python. At first, the datasets have to be read from data frames and different operations can easily be subjected to these columns.

Practice data set – Loan Prediction Problem

The following is the description of variables:

```
VARIABLE DESCRIPTIONS:

Variable                Description

Loan_ID                 Unique Loan ID

Gender                  Male/ Female

Married                 Applicant married (Y/N)

Dependents              Number of dependents

Education               Applicant Education (Graduate/ Under Graduat
e)

Self_Employed           Self employed (Y/N)

ApplicantIncome         Applicant income

CoapplicantIncome       Coapplicant income

LoanAmount              Loan amount in thousands

Loan_Amount_Term        Term of loan in months

Credit_History          credit history meets guidelines

Property_Area           Urban/ Semi Urban/ Rural

Loan_Status             Loan approved (Y/N)
```

First, start iPython interface in Inline Pylab mode by typing the command below on the terminal:

```
ipython notebook --pylab=inline
```

Import libraries and data set

This chapter will use the following python libraries:

- NumPy

- Matplotlib

- Pandas

Once you have imported the library, you can move on and read the dataset using a function read_csv(). Below is how the code will look till this point.

```
import pandas as pd
import numpy as np
import matplotlib as plt
%matplotlib inline
#Reading the dataset in a dataframe using Pandas
df = pd.read_csv("/home/kunal/Downloads/Loan_Prediction/train.csv")
```

Notice that the dataset is stored in

"/home/kunal/Downloads/Loan_Prediction/train.csv"

Once you read the dataset, you can decide to check a few top rows by using the **function head().**

Next, you can check at the summary of numerical fields by using the **describe () function.**

Distribution analysis

Since you are familiar with the basic features of data, this is the time to look at the distribution of different variables. Let's begin with numeric variables-ApplicantIncome and LoanAmount.

First, type the commands below to plot the histogram of ApplicantIncome.

```
df['ApplicantIncome'].hist(bins=50)
```

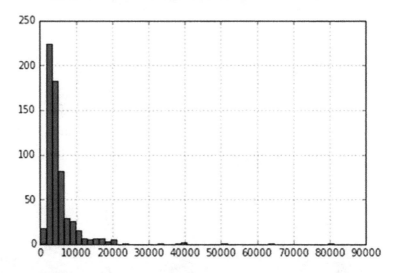

Notice that there are a few extreme values. This is why 50 bins are needed to represent the distribution clearly.

The next thing to focus on is the box plot. The box plot for fare is plotted by:

```
df.boxplot(column='ApplicantIncome')
```

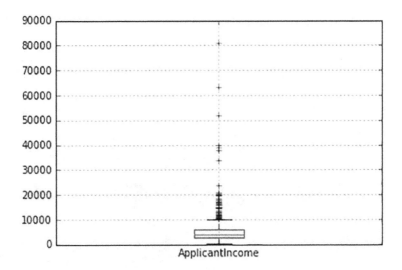

ApplicantIncome

This is just a tip of an iceberg when it comes data processing in Python.

Let's look at:

Techniques for Preprocessing Data in Python

Here are the best techniques for Data Preprocessing in Python.

1. Rescaling Data

When you work with data that has different scales, you need to rescale the properties to have the same scale. The properties are rescaled between the range 0 to 1 and refer to it as normalization. To achieve this, the MinMaxScaler class from scikit-learn is used. For example:

```
>>> import pandas, scipy, numpy
>>> from sklearn.preprocessing import MinMaxScaler
>>> df=pandas.read_csv( 'http://archive.ics.uci.edu/ml/machine-learning-databases/wine-quality/winequality-red.csv ',sep=';')
>>> array=df.values
>>> #Separating data into input and output components
>>> x=array[:,0:8]
>>> y=array[:,8]
>>> scaler=MinMaxScaler(feature_range=(0,1))
>>> rescaledX=scaler.fit_transform(x)
>>> numpy.set_printoptions(precision=3) #Setting precision for the output
>>> rescaledX[0:5,:]
```

```
>>> rescaledX[0:5,:]
array([[0.248, 0.397, 0.   , 0.068, 0.107, 0.141, 0.099, 0.568],
       [0.283, 0.521, 0.   , 0.116, 0.144, 0.338, 0.216, 0.494],
       [0.283, 0.438, 0.04 , 0.096, 0.134, 0.197, 0.17 , 0.509],
       [0.584, 0.11 , 0.56 , 0.068, 0.105, 0.225, 0.191, 0.582],
       [0.248, 0.397, 0.   , 0.068, 0.107, 0.141, 0.099, 0.568]])
```

After rescaling, you get the values between 0 and 1. By rescaling data, it confirms the use of neural networks, optimization algorithms as well as those which have distance measures such as the k-nearest neighbors.

2. Normalizing Data

In the following task, you rescale every observation to a specific length of 1. For this case, you use the Normalizer class. Here is an example:

```
>>> from sklearn.preprocessing import Normalizer
>>> scaler=Normalizer().fit(x)
>>> normalizedX=scaler.transform(x)
>>> normalizedX[0:5,:]
```

```
>>> normalizedX[0:5,:]
array([[2.024e-01, 1.914e-02, 0.000e+00, 5.196e-02, 2.079e-03, 3.008e-01,
        9.299e-01, 2.729e-02],
       [1.083e-01, 1.222e-02, 0.000e+00, 3.611e-02, 1.361e-03, 3.472e-01,
        9.306e-01, 1.385e-02],
       [1.377e-01, 1.342e-02, 7.061e-04, 4.060e-02, 1.624e-03, 2.648e-01,
        9.533e-01, 1.760e-02],
       [1.767e-01, 4.416e-03, 8.833e-03, 2.997e-02, 1.183e-03, 2.681e-01,
        9.464e-01, 1.574e-02],
       [2.024e-01, 1.914e-02, 0.000e+00, 5.196e-02, 2.079e-03, 3.008e-01,
        9.299e-01, 2.729e-02]])
```

3. Binarizing Data

If you use the binary threshold, it is possible to change the data and make the value above it to be 1 while those that are equal to or fall below it, 0. For this task, you use the Binarized class.

```
>>> from sklearn.preprocessing import Binarizer
>>> binarizer=Binarizer(threshold=0.0).fit(x)
>>> binaryX=binarizer.transform(x)
>>> binaryX[0:5,:]
```

```
>>> binaryX[0:5,:]
array([[1., 1., 0., 1., 1., 1., 1., 1.],
       [1., 1., 0., 1., 1., 1., 1., 1.],
       [1., 1., 1., 1., 1., 1., 1., 1.],
       [1., 1., 1., 1., 1., 1., 1., 1.],
       [1., 1., 0., 1., 1., 1., 1., 1.]])
```

As you can see, the python code will label 0 overall values equal to or less than 0, and label 1 over the rest.

4. Mean Removal

This is where you remove mean from each property to center it on zero.

5. One Hot Encoding

When you deal with a few and scattered numerical values, you might need to store them before you can carry out the One Hot Encoding. For the k-distinct values, you can change the feature into a k-dimensional vector that has a single value of 1 and 0 for the remaining values.

```
>>> from sklearn.preprocessing import OneHotEncoder
>>> encoder=OneHotEncoder()
>>> encoder.fit([[0,1,6,2],
[1,5,3,5],
[2,4,2,7],
[1,0,4,2]
])
```

6. Label Encoding

Sometimes labels can be words or numbers. If you want to label the training data, you need to use words to increase its readability. Label encoding changes word labels into numbers to allow algorithms to operate on them. Here's an example:

```
>>> from sklearn.preprocessing import LabelEncoder
>>> label_encoder=LabelEncoder()
>>> input_classes=['Havells','Philips','Syska','Eveready','Lloyd']
>>> label_encoder.fit(input_classes)
```

Chapter 4

Regression

Linear regression
Linear regression is one of the most popular types of predictive analysis. Linear regression involves the following two things:

1. Do the predictor variables forecast the results of an outcome variable accurately?

2. Which particular variable are key predictors of the final variable, and in what standard does it impact the outcome variable?

Naming variables
The regression's dependent variable has many different names. Some names include outcome variable, criterion variable, and many others. The independent variable can be called exogenous variable or repressors.

Functions of the regression analysis
1. Trend Forecasting

2. Determine the strength of predictors

3. Predict an effect

Breaking down regression
There are two basic states of regression-linear and multiple regression. Although there are different methods for complex data and analysis. Linear regression contains an independent variable to help forecast the

outcome of a dependent variable. On the other hand, multiple regression has two or more independent variables to assist in predicting a result.

Regression is very useful to financial and investment institutions because it is used to predict the sales of a particular product or company based on the previous sales and GDP growth among many other factors. The capital pricing model is one of the most common regression models applied in the finance. The example below describes formulae used in the linear and multiple regression.

```
Linear Regression: Y = a + bX + u
Multiple Regression: Y = a + b1X1 + b2X2 + b3X3 + ... + btXt + u
In this case:
Y = variable which you want to predict (dependent variable)
X = variable which you are using to predict Y (independent variable)
a = the intercept
b = the slope
u = regression residual
```

Choosing the best regression model
Selecting the right linear regression model can be very hard and confusing. Trying to model it with a sample data cannot make it easier. This section reviews some of the most popular statistical methods which one can use to choose models, challenges that you might come across, and lists some practical advice to use to select the correct regression model.

It always begins with a researcher who would like to expand the relationship between the response variable and predictors. The research team that is accorded with the responsibility to perform investigation essentially measures a lot of variables but only has a few in the model. The analysts will make efforts to reduce the variables that are different and apply the ones which have an accurate relationship. As time moves on, the analysts continue to add more models.

Statistical methods to use to find the best regression model

If you want a great model in regression, then it is important to take into consideration the type of variables which you want to test as well as other variables which can affect the response.

Modified R-squared and Predicted R-squared.

Your model should have a higher modified and predicted R-squared values. The statistics are shown below help eliminate critical issues which revolve around R-squared.

- The adjusted R squared increases once a new term improves the model.

- Predicted R-squared belongs to the cross-validation that helps define the manner in which your model can generalize remaining data sets.

P-values for the Predictors

When it comes to regression, a low value of P denotes statistically significant terms. The term "Reducing the model" refers to the process of factoring in all candidate predictors contained in a model.

Stepwise regression

This is an automated technique which can select important predictors found in the exploratory stages of creating a model.

Real World Challenges

There are different statistical approaches for choosing the best model. However, complications still exist.

- The best model happens when the variables are measured by the study.

- The sample data could be unusual because of the type of data collection method. A false positive and false negative process happens when you handle samples.

94

- If you deal with enough models, you'll get variables that are significant but only correlated by chance.

- P-values can be different depending on the specific terms found in the model.

- Studies have discovered that the best subset regression and stepwise regression can't select the correct model.

Finding the correct Regression Model

Theory

Perform research done by other experts and reference it into your model. It is important that before you start regression analysis, you should develop ideas about the most significant variables. Developing something based on outcome from other people eases the process of collecting data.

Complexity

You may think that complex problems need a complex model. Well, that is not the case because studies show that even a simple model can provide an accurate prediction. Once there is a model with the same explanatory potential, the simplest model is likely to be a perfect choice. You just need to start with a simple model as you slowly advance the complexity of the model.

How to calculate the accuracy of the predictive model

There are different ways in which you can compute the accuracy of your model. Some of these methods include:

1. You divide the dataset into a test and training data set. Next, build the model based on the training set and apply the test set as a holdout sample to measure your trained model with the test data. The next thing to do is to compare the predicted values using actual values by computing the error by using measures

like the "Mean Absolute Percent Error" (MAPE). If your MAPE is less than 10%, then you have a great model.

2. Another method is to calculate the "Confusion Matrix" to the computer False Positive Rate and False Negative Rate. These measures will allow a person to choose whether to accept the model or not. If you consider the cost of the errors, it becomes a critical stage of your decision whether to reject or accept the model.

3. Computing Receiver Operating Characteristic Curve (ROC) or the Lift Chart or Area under the curve (AUC) are other methods that you can use to decide on whether to reject or accept a model.

Chapter 5

Classification

Classification refers to the process of predicting the class of a particular data point. Classes are referred to as labels, targets, or categories. Classification predictive modeling is the procedure of estimating a mapping function (f) from input variables (X) to discrete output variables (y).

Let's take the example of spam detection in email service providers which can be selected as a classification challenge. This is an example of a binary classification

because there are just 2 classes: a spam and not a spam. A classifier takes advantage of training data to understand the way a specific input of variables is associated with a particular class. In the following example, known spam and non-spam emails should be used as the training data.

When the classifier is accurately trained, you can use it to detect unknown email.

Classification is a field of supervised learning where targets come with the input data. There are many areas in real life where classification is applied. Some of these areas include medical diagnosis, credit approval, target marketing, and many more.

The classification has two types of learners.

1. Lazy learners

Lazy learners hold training data and wait till the time when a testing data arrives. Once the data arrives, classification is performed depending on the common data found in the training data. When you compare it to eager learners, lazy learners have a minimum time of training. However, more time is required in prediction. An example includes k-nearest neighbor and case-based reasoning which we shall look later in the chapter.

2. Eager learners

With eager learners, the classification model is created with respect to the type of training data before getting data for classification. It should be able to dedicate a single hypothesis that handles the whole instance space. Because of the construction of the model, eager learners will consume more training time and minimum time during prediction. Example of eager learners includes Artificial Neural Networks, Naive Bayes and Decision Tree.

Classification Algorithms

There are many different kinds of classification algorithms developed, however, it is hard to pick on one which is better than the other. This is because of a few factors such as the application and nature of the existing data set. For instance, if you have linearly separable classes, the linear classifiers such as Logistic regression, Fisher's linear discriminant can execute complex models.

Decision Tree

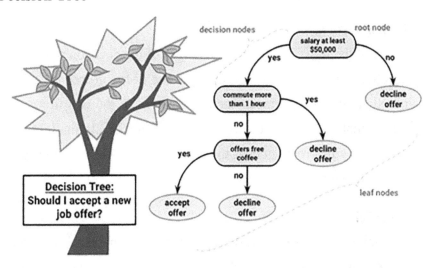

A decision tree creates regression models and classification models just like a tree structure. This tree works with the same concept as the if-then rule set that is mutually exclusive and exhaustive for classification. Rules are learned sequentially by applying the training data one at a time. Every time a rule is learned, the tuples which the rules handles are deleted. This process is repeated on the training set until a meeting termination condition is attained.

The tree is built through a technique called top-down recursive divide-and-conquer manner. All the features must be categorical. Nonetheless, they need to be discretized in advance. With a decision tree, it is very easy for overfitting to take place. Overfitting will produce many branches which may indicate problems of noise and outliers. In an overfitted model, the performance is very poor on the unseen data although it provides the correct performance on training data.

However, this is can be avoided by applying pre-pruning. Pre-pruning shall stop the tree construction early or post-pruning which eliminates branches from a complete tree.

Pros of Decision trees

1. Transparency

This is one of the most important advantages of the decision tree model. Unlike other models of the decision tree, the decision tree reveals all possible alternatives and traces each alternative to the end in a single view. This makes it easy to compare the different alternatives. The application of different nodes to represent user-defined decisions increases transparency in decision making.

2. Specificity

Another major advantage of the decision tree in the analysis is the ability to allocate a given value to a problem and outcomes of every decision. This is important because it helps minimize vagueness in the decision making. Every possible case from a decision tree discovers a representation using a clear fork and node. This allows one to see all solutions in a clear view. The inclusion of monetary values to decision tree reveals the costs and benefits of taking a different course of action.

3. Ease of use

The decision tree has a graphical representation of the problem and different alternatives in an easy and simple way to help any person understand without asking for an explanation.

4. Comprehensive nature

The decision tree is one of the best predictive models because it has a comprehensive analysis of the results of every possible decision. That can include what the decision leads to, if it finishes in uncertainty or whether it results to new issues which the process may require repetition.

5. They implicitly perform feature selection.

6. Decision trees can deal with categorical and numerical data.

7. Users have little to do with data preparation.

8. Nonlinear relationships between parameters cannot affect the performance.

Disadvantages of Decision trees

1. There are times when decision trees can be unstable because of the little variations in the data that may lead to a totally different tree generated.

2. The greedy algorithm cannot prove that it will return a universally optimal decision tree. This can be solved by training multiple trees where the samples and features have been randomly sampled with replacement.

3. Learners of the decision tree can build advanced trees that don't generalize the data.

4. Decision tree learners can be biased if there are classes which dominate.

For that reason, it is advised to balance the data set before fitting with the decision tree.

K-Nearest Neighbor (KNN)

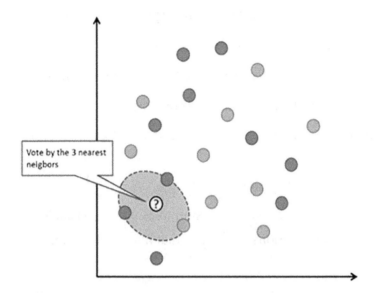

The k-nearest Neighbor belongs to the lazy learning algorithm which holds all instances that match to training data points in n-dimensional space. In case there is an unknown discrete data, it has to make an analysis of the nearest k number of instances saved and display the most popular class as the prediction. For the real-valued data, it has to return the mean of k-nearest neighbors.

In the case of the distance-weighted nearest neighbor algorithm, it measures the weight of every k-nearest neighbor based on their distance by applying the query below.

$$w \equiv \frac{1}{d(x_q, x_i)^2}$$

Distance calculating query

Typically, KNN is very strong to noisy data because it averages the k-nearest neighbors.

Pros of KNN
- A simple algorithm to explain and understand
- It doesn't make any assumptions about data.
- It has a higher accuracy that is not comparable to other better-supervised learning models.
- It is versatile for classification and regression.

Cons of KNN
- Calls for a higher memory requirement
- It is computationally expensive since the algorithm has all the training data.

Quick features of KNN
- This algorithm holds the whole training dataset that uses as a representation.
- It doesn't learn any model.
- It performs timely predictions by calculating the similarity between sample input and instance training.

Where Can You Apply K-means

K-means is used with data that is numeric, continuous and has a small dimension. Imagine an instance where you would like to group similar items from a randomly spread collection of things such as k-means. This list has a few interesting areas where you can apply K-means

1. Classification of documents

Clustering of documents in numerous categories depends on topics, tags, and the content of the document. This is a normal classification problem and k-means is a great algorithm for this function. The original document processing is important when you want to replace every document as a sector and applies the frequency term to use terms which classify the document. The vectors of the document have to be clustered so that they can select similarity in document groups.

2. Delivery store Optimization

If you want to improve the process of delivery, you'll need to enhance it by applying drones and integrating k-means algorithm to determine the optimal number of launch locations and a genetic algorithm to compute the route of the truck.

3. Fantasy League Stat Analysis

To analyze the stats of a player is one of the most critical features of the sporting world. With the rapid rise of competition, machine learning has an important function to offer here. As a great exercise, if you want to build a fantasy draft team and select similar players, k-means is a great option.

4. Rideshare Data analysis

Information about Uber is available to the public. This dataset has an extensive size of valuable data about transit time, traffic, peak pickup localities, and many more. If you analyze this particular data, you will get insight into the urban traffic patterns and help plan for the cities in the future.

5. Cyber-profiling criminals

This is the process of gathering data from people and groups to select important links. The concept behind cyber-profiling is extracted from criminal histories that provide information about investigation division to help categorize criminals present at the crime.

6. Automatic clustering of IT Alerts

Extensive enterprise in IT infrastructure technology like network generates huge volumes of alert messages. Since alert messages refer to operational issues, it has to be manually screened for categorization. Data clustering can help provide insight into alert categories and the mean time to repair and support predictions.

7. Identify crime localities

Since data associated to crime is present in specific city localities, the type of crime, the area of the crime, and the relation between the two can provide quality insight into the most crime-prone areas in the city or a locality.

Artificial Neural Network

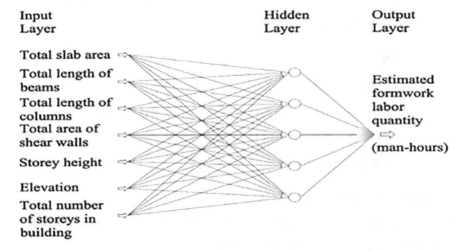

Artificial Neural Network describes a set of connected input/output where every connection is linked to a particular weight. In the learning phase, the network adjusts the weights so that it can predict the right class label of input tuples.

There are a lot of network architectures present now. Some of them include the Feed-forward, Recurrent, Convolutional, etc. The correct architecture depends on the model application. In most cases, the feed-

105

forward models provide a reasonably accurate result and mostly for image processing applications.

There can be many hidden layers in a model based on the complexity of the function that is to be wrapped by the model. If you have a lot of hidden layers, it will facilitate the modeling of complex relationships like deep neural networks.

However, the presence of many hidden layers increases the time it takes to train and adjust weights. Another drawback is the poor interpretability when compared to other models such as Decision Trees.

Despite this, ANN has performed well in the majority of the real-world applications. It has an intensive persistence to noisy data and can categorize untrained patterns. Generally, ANN works better with continuous-valued inputs and outputs.

Pros of ANN

•   It stores information in the whole network. For example, traditional programming information is kept in the whole network, and not in a database. This means that loss of certain information in a given place does not stop the network functions.

•   It has fault tolerance. The destruction of one or more cells of ANN doesn't affect it from producing input. Therefore, this specific feature causes the network to be fault tolerant.

•   It can work with incomplete knowledge. Once the ANN training is over, the data can produce output using incomplete information. The loss of performance, in this case, will depend on the missing information.

•   ANN has the ability to make machine learning.

- It has a parallel processing capability. The ANN neural networks feature a numerical strength that does more than one job at the same time.

Disadvantages of ANN

- It depends on the hardware. ANN need processors which contain parallel processing power based on their structure. For this case, the realization of the device is dependent.

- The determination of the correct network structure. Often, there is no fixed rule to use to determine the structure of artificial neural networks. The right network structure is attained through trial and error.

- The duration of the network is not known. The network is limited to a particular value of the error on the sample means which the training is completed. This value does not generate an optimum result.

- There are unexplained characteristics of the network. It is one of the major problems of ANN. If an ANN generates a probing solution, it doesn't show any hint. This always reduces trust in the network.

Naïve Bayes

The Naïve Bayes algorithm is a probabilistic classifier which was driven by the Bayes theorem. This is based on a simple assumption where attributes are conditionally independent.

$$P(X \mid C_i) = \prod_{k=1}^{n} P(x_k \mid C_i) = P(x_1 \mid C_i) \times P(x_2 \mid C_i) \times ... \times P(x_n \mid C_i)$$

The classification works by extracting the maximum posterior that is the maximal $P(C_i \mid X)$ with the above-stated assumption working. This assumption always reduces the computational cost by measuring the computational cost. Although the assumption fails many times because the properties are dependent. Despite this, the Naïve Bayes has continued to work so well.

This is a simple algorithm to implement and improve outcomes that have been generated in most instances. It is possible for it to be scaled into massive datasets because it assumes a linear time.

Pros of Naïve Bayes

- It is simple and easy to implement.

- It requires minimal training data.

- It handles continuous and discrete data.

- It can develop probabilistic predictions.

- It is highly scalable.

Cons of Naïve Bayes

- It makes a robust assumption regarding the shape of the data distribution.

- There are challenges related to data scarcity.

- The issue of continuous features that requires a binning procedure to make them discrete.

Classification Accuracy Metrics
This refers to the ratio of the number of correct predictions to the general number of input samples.

$$Accuracy = \frac{Number\ of\ Correct\ predictions}{Total\ number\ of\ predictions\ made}$$

It works better when the number of samples which belong to each class is equal. Classification accuracy is the best but provides a false notion of attaining high accuracy.

The major problem emerges when the cost of misclassification of minor class samples is high. If you are to handle a rare but dangerous disease, the cost of not diagnosing the disease of a sick individual is very high compared to the cost of testing a healthy person.

Logarithmic Loss

This operates well for multi-class classification. When you work with Log Loss, the classifier has to allocate probability for every class. For example, if you have N samples of M classes, you can compute the Log Loss as follows:

$$LogarithmicLoss = \frac{-1}{N} \sum_{i=1}^{N} \sum_{j=1}^{M} y_{ij} * \log(p_{ij})$$

where,

y_ij, indicates whether sample i belongs to class j or not

p_ij, indicates the probability of sample i belonging to class j

Confusion Matrix

Confusion matrix as the name suggests creates a matrix as the output and explains the complete performance of a model.

Suppose you have a binary classification problem. Then there are some samples which belong to two classes: YES or NO. Additionally, you have your own classifier that can predict a class for a particular input sample. If the following model is tested on 165 samples, the following result is obtained.

n=165	Predicted: NO	Predicted: YES
Actual: NO	50	10
Actual: YES	5	100

There are four major terms:

1. True Positives. This is where our prediction was YES and final outcome YES.

2. True Negatives. This is where our prediction was NO and final outcome NO.

3. False Positives. In this case, the prediction was YES but the final outcome was NO.

4. False Negatives. In this scenario, the prediction was NO but the final outcome was YES.

Area Under the Curve

This is one of the most widely applied metrics for evaluation. It is applied in binary application problems.

Other metrics include:

- Mean absolute error
- Mean squared error

Chapter 6

Clustering

Clustering is the process of gathering entities with similar characteristics together. This technique belongs to unsupervised machine learning whose target is to identify similarities in the data point and group the same data points together.

Why apply Clustering?

By grouping similar entities in one place allows one to identify the attributes of different groups. In other words, this generates insight into the underlying patterns of various groups. There are countless application areas of grouping unlabeled data.

For example, it is possible to select different groups of customers and market every group differently to take advantage of the revenue. Another example may include grouping documents together that belong to similar topics. Additionally, clustering is used to reduce the dimensionality of the data when you handle various copious variables.

3 Main Types of Clustering

Partitioned-based clustering

The phrase cluster doesn't have an accurate definition. A cluster describes a set of points whereby any point in the cluster is close to any other point in the cluster than a point absent in the cluster. Sometimes, a threshold is used to define all points in a cluster close to one another.

A partitioning method will first create an original set of K-partitions where k- parameter is the number of partitions to construct. Next, it applies an iterative relocation approach which tries to enhance the partitioning by shifting objects from one group to another. These clustering techniques help generate a one-level partitioning of data points. There are various partitioning-based clustering like K-means, fuzzy C-, means, and K-medoids. This section will look at K-mean clustering.

K-mean Clustering

1. It begins with K as the input. This refers to the number of clusters that you want to find. Assign K-centroids in random positions in your space.

2. Now, if you use the Euclidean distance between data points and centroids, allocate each data point to the cluster close to it.

3. Re-compute the cluster centers as a mean of data points allocated to it.

4. Repeat 2 and 3 till there are no more changes to happen.

You might be wondering how you can select the value of K.

One method is the "Elbow" that is used to define an optimal number of clusters. In this case, you'll run the range of K values and plot the "percentage of variance explained," on Y-axis and "K" on the "X" axis.

In the diagram below, more clusters have been added after 3. These additional clusters affect the display of the model. The first cluster adds more information, and at a certain point, the marginal gain will start to drop.

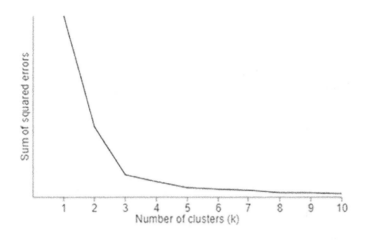

Hierarchical clustering

With the Hierarchical clustering, it begins by assigning all data points to belong to its own cluster. Just as the name implies, it creates the hierarchy and in the next step, it integrates the two closest data point and combines it together into a single cluster.

1. Allocate every data point to its cluster.

2. Determine the closest pair of the cluster by applying the Euclidean distance and combine it into a single cluster.

3. Determine the distance between two nearest clusters and integrate them until when all items are grouped into a single cluster.

In the next method, you can choose the best number of clusters by identifying which vertical lines are cut by a horizontal line without affecting a cluster and deals with the maximum distance.

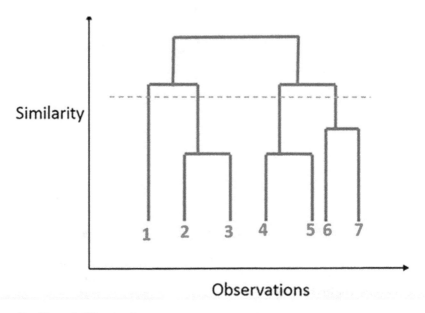

Density Based Clustering

The basic concept underlying density-based clustering technique is extracted from a human perception clustering method. For example, if you look at the images below, you should be able to see four clusters plus different points of noise.

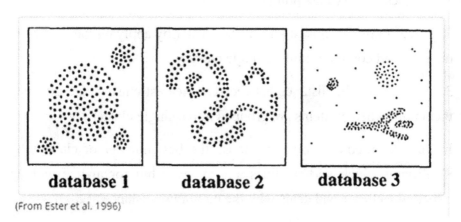

database 1   database 2   database 3

(From Ester et al. 1996)

As shown in the above image, the clusters are dense regions in the data space that are delineated by regions of a lower density point. In short, the density of points in a cluster is somehow higher compared to the density of points located outside the cluster.

The density-based clustering algorithm depends on an intuitive perception of "clusters" and "noise". The point is that for every cluster, the neighborhood of a particular radius should have at least a minimum.

The most important parameters are needed for DBSCAN include ("eps") and minimum points ("MinPts"). The parameter eps determine the radius of the neighborhood around close to a point x. The parameter MinPts describes the minimum number of neighbors in the "eps" radius.

Any point x that exists in the dataset that has a count higher than or equal to MinPts is identified as a core point.

Customer Segmentation with Cluster analysis

The customer base of a company can have thousands, if not millions, of different unique persons. Marketing, to most of these people, presents a big problem because if you attempt to market to everybody, the message can be ambiguous. However, building a marketing plan which attracts every individual is not normal.

Why customer segments are important

Customer segments will make you understand the patterns which distinguish your customers. Below are some important ideas that you can achieve with segmentation analysis.

- Enhanced understanding of the customer needs and wants. This can lead to improved sales and customer satisfaction.

- Create products that appeal to different customer segments.

- Companies cannot fulfill all possible customers all the time. By applying segmentation procedure, companies have the ability to concentrate on fulfilling those segments which they examine to be the best attractions for their products.

- Build loyal relationships.

While you can analyze your own customer base, soon it shall be clear that there are different groups that have customized requirements. This allows you to build a deeper understanding of your customers and find out what makes them tick.

It is no gem that a customer is always more profitable compared to others. However, to be profitable, businesses should have a better understanding of the way profitability relates to customer segmentation. Discovering the difference between customers will permit one to personalize your method to the desires of the customer segments.

Customer segmentation describes the practice of categorizing a customer base into different groups of individuals similar in a given way. Customer segments are often determined based on similarities such as personal characteristics, behaviors, and preferences. By understanding your customers and their differences, it becomes one of the most important stages of measuring the customers' relationship.

How to segment
Segmentation doesn't need to be very complex. For a small organization or company, it can be about discovering that you have two or three unique customer types who have different needs. Some popular methods used to segment customers consist of:

- Demographic
- Behavioral
- Psychographic
- Geographic

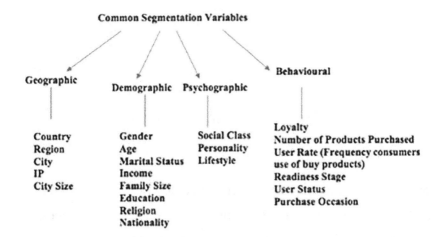

Common Segmentation Variables

Geographic	Demographic	Psychographic	Behavioural
Country	Gender	Social Class	Loyalty
Region	Age	Personality	Number of Products Purchased
City	Marital Status	Lifestyle	User Rate (Frequency consumers
IP	Income		use of buy products)
City Size	Family Size		Readiness Stage
	Education		User Status
	Religion		Purchase Occasion
	Nationality		

There are different ways which you can apply when it comes to segmentation of a market. One of the methods that are accurate and statistically valid is the application of cluster analysis.

Chapter 7

Recommender Systems

Most e-commerce and retail companies are taking advantage of the massive potential of data to boost sales by implementing a Recommender system on their particular websites.

These systems focus on suggesting to the user's items that they may like or have interest in.

The data needed for recommendation engines comes from explicit user ratings to watch a movie or listen to a song from implicit search engine purchase histories and queries. Sites such as YouTube, Spotify, and Netflix have data to use to recommend playlists.

Pros of using recommendation systems
Companies which apply the Recommender system concentrate on raising the sales due to the personalized offers and improved customer experience.

Recommendations usually increase searches and make it easy for users to access content which they are interested in, and surprise them with offers that they have never searched before.

What is interesting is that companies can now gain and retain customers by sending out email links to new offers that fulfill the interests of their profiles.

By creating an added advantage to users through suggesting products and systems, it creates a great feeling among buyers. This is a great thing because it will allow companies to stay ahead of their competitors.

Types of Recommender Systems

Recommender systems operate with two types of information:

- User-item interactions

- Characteristic information

This helps us reach the first classification of recommender systems. This includes a content-based system that has a characteristic information and collaborative filtering which depends on user-item interactions. The hybrid systems shall combine both information with the goal to avoid problems generated when you work with only one specific type.

Content-based Systems

Content-based systems are built from the idea of applying the content of each product for purposes of recommendation. Below are some pros and cons of the content-based recommender system.

Pros

- It is simple to create a more transparent system. You use the same content to describe the recommendations.

- Content representations are different and they open up the options to apply unique approaches like text processing techniques, inferences, and semantic information.

- In case of items have enough descriptions, there is no need for the "new item problem".

Cons

- The content-based RecSys seem to over-specialize. They will suggest items similar to that which is already consumed, with a notion to create a "filter bubble".

Another issue is that new users don't have a defined profile not unless they are explicitly requested for information. Despite this, it is very simple to add new items to the system. You simply require to allocate them a group based on their features.

Three principal components

- A content Analyzer-This classifies items using a given type of representation.

- A profile Learner-It creates a profile which represents every user's preference.

- A filtering Component-It accepts all the inputs and creates a list of recommendations for every user.

How content is represented

The content of a particular item is abstract and provides more options. You can use many different variables. For instance, for a book, you can include the genre, author, the text of the book and many other factors.

Once you know which content you will factor. You need to convert all the data into a vector space model, which is an algebraic representation of text documents.

You perform this using a Bag of Words model which represents documents disregarding the sequence of words. In this particular model, every document appears like a bag with some words. Therefore, this method will permit word modeling with respect to dictionaries, where every bag has some words from the dictionary.

An exact implementation of a Bag of Words is the TF-IDF representation. In full, TF stands for Term Frequency and IDF stands for Inverse Document Frequency. This particular model combines the significance of the word in the document with the significance of the world in the corpus.

This was just a general aspect of Content-based recommendation engines. It is important to recognize that a Bag of Words representation doesn't factor in the context of words. If it is necessary to include that, Semantic Content Representation becomes useful. Below are two options that one has, just in case you want to know more about it.

Option 1: Explicit Semantic Representation
- Wordnet

- ConceptNet

- Ontologies for Semantic Representation

Option 2: Infer Semantic Representation
- Latent Dirichlet Allocation

- Latent Semantic Indexing

Collaborative filtering systems
These types of recommendation engine implement user interactions to evaluate items of interest. You can visualize the set of interactions using a matrix where every entry (I, j) represents the interactions between user i and item j. One way of looking at collaborative filtering is to look at it as a generalization of regression and classification. In the following case, you aim to predict a variable directly which depends on other variables in the collaborative filtering.

Visualizing a problem as a matrix allows us not only to predict the values of a unique column but also help us predict the values of any entry.

Techniques to apply in collaborative filtering
There is a lot of research that has been done on collaborative filtering, and most common techniques depend on low-dimensional factor models that depend on matrix factorization. The CF techniques are divided into 2 types:

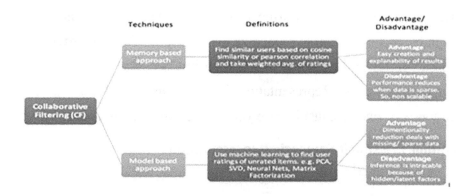

Types of collaborative filtering approaches. Reference: Wikipedia

Below is a brief discussion of some of these techniques

1. Memory-based technique
This approach can further be divided into two sections: User-item filtering and item-item filtering. The user-item filtering selects a given user, searches for users that are similar to the user depending on the similarity of the ratings, and suggest items that the same users recommended. On the other hand, item-item filtering will identify an item, search users who liked an item and look for other products that the same users liked. In other words, this approach takes items and displays the items as recommendations.

The major difference of memory-based technique from the model-based techniques is that no parameter is learned using gradient descent.

2. Model-based approach

In this particular approach, CF models are created using machine learning algorithms to predict the ratings of items unrelated to the user.

Content-Based Filtering

This system will suggest an item to users depending on their past history.

The greatest advantage of content-based filtering is that it can start to suggest items immediately information related to items is available.

A content-based system will work with information which the user provides, this can be explicitly or implicitly. Depending on data, a user profile is created that provides a lot of inputs or takes actions about recommendations.

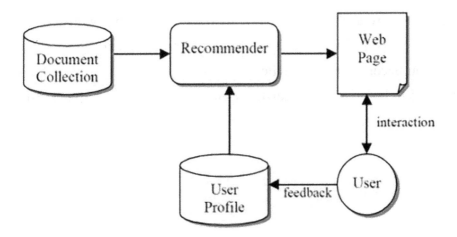

Conclusion

With some knowledge of basic Python, machine learning skills, and Python libraries, you are now set to launch your first machine learning project with Python. Consider learning the open-source Python libraries. The scientific Python libraries will help you complete easy machine learning tasks. However, the choice of some of these libraries can be completely subjective and highly debatable by many people in the industry.

All in all, we recommend you to start by exploring Scikit-learn library. Make sure you are familiar with its concepts and how to use it. Once you are done with it, you can dive deep into advanced machine learning topics such as complex data transformation and vector machines.

Just like how a child learns how to walk is the same with learning Machine Learning with Python. You need to practice many times before you can become better. Practice different algorithms and use different datasets to improve your knowledge and overall problem-solving skills.

www.ingramcontent.com/pod-product-compliance
Lightning Source LLC
Chambersburg PA
CBHW071220050326
40689CB00011B/2387